BULLYING

~ Being Prepared to Intervene in Ways That Make a Difference ~

A COMPREHENSIVE GUIDE
for
PARENTS, TEACHERS & MENTORS

by
The Master Method Academy

Foreword by
Grandmaster Marco Sies
7-Time World Champion

CONTENTS

Acknowledgments   5

Dedication   7

Foreword   9
Grandmaster Marco Sies, Founder of The Master Method
Academies

Introduction   13

Getting Started   21

1. Understanding Bullying   23
   A Closer Look at What Bullying Is, the Types, and Why It Happens

2. The Power Of Adults   51
   *Developing Knowledge and Skills to Address Bullying & Providing
   Meaningful Support to Children*

3. Confidence Development   67
   *A Key to Help Children Feel Worthy and Capable, No Matter What
   Others Say or Do*

4. Empathy & Resilience   79
   *Helping Kids Overcome Bullying with Confidence, Awareness, and
   Mental Self-Defense Strategies*

5. Intervention Strategies   97
   *Taking Meaningful Action to Support Bullied Children Wherever it
   Occurs*

6. Case Studies & Examples   119
   Success Stories of Intervention and Support at School and at Home

7. Parent, Teacher & Community Collaboration   133
   *Helping Children Process Emotions & Rebuild Confidence Through
   Love, Reassurance & Positive Action*

8. Digital Safety & Cyberbullying   147
   *How to Help Your Children When They are Bullied—Even When it
   Occurs Online*

9. Mental Health, Inclusion & Long-Term Support   155
   *Helping Children Overcome Bullying Related Pain, Low Self-
   Esteem and Self-Doubt*

10. Final Thoughts   167
    A United Path Forward to Break the Cycle of Bullying

Master Method Academy Books   173
References   175
Support Directory   179

ACKNOWLEDGMENTS

The creation of this guide was made possible through the wisdom, inspiration, and dedication of so many individuals and organizations who share the important mission of creating safer, more compassionate environments for every child.

To the students and families who have shared their personal experiences with vulnerability and courage—your stories gave this book its heart. Your voices remind us of the urgency and importance of this work and you inspire us to keep working.

To the teachers, school counselors, administrators, and staff on the front lines of education and advocacy—thank you for your daily commitment to nurturing emotional safety and empowering young minds.

To the researchers and thought leaders in bullying prevention, mental health, and social-emotional learning—your groundbreaking work laid the foundation for the evidence-based strategies shared in these pages.

A heartfelt thank you to Grandmaster Marco Sies, whose powerful personal story and lifelong dedication to building confidence in children inspired the inception of this book and so much of its core message. Your example of resilience, overcoming adversity, and your dedication to building our youth continues to change lives.

Special thanks to The Master Method Academy's team of instructors, educators, and administrative staff whose tireless efforts develop and empower youth through leadership training, martial arts and community outreach. Your impact extends far beyond the walls of the academy. It touches the hearts of so many all over the world.

To our collaborators and contributors, including child psychologists, education specialists, school policy advocates, and parent leaders— thank you for offering your wisdom, your care, and your time.

And finally, to every parent, mentor, and adult role model who has chosen to be a positive force in a child's life—we are truly grateful to you. Your actions, words, and presence shape the future in powerful ways.

Together, we can help develop confidence, empathy, stand up to bullying, and stop the cycle. We can create a world where every child feels safe, supported, and loved.

With deepest gratitude,
Julie Sies
Academy Director & CEO
The Master Method Academy

Dedication

To every child who has ever felt invisible, unheard, or alone because of
bullying—
this book is for you.

May you always know your worth, find your voice,
and discover the strength within you to rise above the storms.

You are not what was done to you.
You are brave.
You are powerful.
You are enough.
You are loved.

And to those who choose kindness, who stand up, speak out, and
reach out—
You are the change the world needs.

FOREWORD

GRANDMASTER MARCO SIES, FOUNDER
OF THE MASTER METHOD ACADEMIES

As a child growing up in Chile, I knew what it meant to feel belittled, scared, and powerless. I was bullied relentlessly for my size, and my darker skin also made me a target of hurtful, hateful comments. Classmates called me "dirty" and "ugly." They laughed at me, repeatedly harassed me, chased me down and threw me in trash cans. They even whipped me with their school uniform ties like an animal. The cruelty felt endless. I began to believe the lies they told me about what I was worth, and some deep scars within me took a very long time to heal.

But something shifted the day I found martial arts. Through my training, I began to rebuild what bullying had broken. The discipline and focus I learned helped me connect with my inner strength. I started walking taller and felt my confidence building—not just physically, but mentally and emotionally. I learned to feel sorry for kids who behaved badly, realizing they were in pain.

I also realized I didn't have to accept the identity others tried to force on me. I had the power to define who I was. And more importantly, I discovered that true and lasting confidence comes from within. Once I found my confidence, I stood up for myself, faced my tormentors, and they never bothered me again.

That discovery didn't just change my life, it became my life's purpose.

For more than three decades, I've committed my life to helping children discover their inner strength and develop the confidence to persevere, overcome challenges, and achieve their dreams. Through The Master Method Academies, and in partnership with schools, families, and communities across the globe, we've built programs that extend far beyond martial arts—programs that teach leadership, goal-setting, personal achievement, and holistic wellness. At the heart of our mission is a foundation of developing strong character and a positive mindset rooted in kindness, compassion, and courage.

Our goal is simple: to help kids develop the tools they need to believe in themselves, overcome challenges, achieve anything they envision, and live lives of kindness and positivity.

This book, Bullying - A Comprehensive Guide for Parents, Teachers, Mentors & Role Models, is a powerful extension of our mission, and is part of a greater initiative to help children, parents, teachers and communities end the cycle of bullying. This book brings together current research and data, expert insights, and practical recommendations to empower the adults in a child's life to become strong allies in the fight against bullying. Drawing from trusted sources and evidence-based practices, it reminds us of the critical role we all play—not only in preventing bullying, but in fostering confidence, empathy, and safer environments where every child feels safe and supported.

I truly believe every child deserves to feel safe, seen, and supported. And I believe that together, we can make that possible.

—*Grandmaster Marco Sies*

7-Time World Champion
Founder, The Master Method Academies
Author, The Mindset Guide for Winners
Nominee, 2025 Positive Impact Book Awards Author of the Year

INTRODUCTION

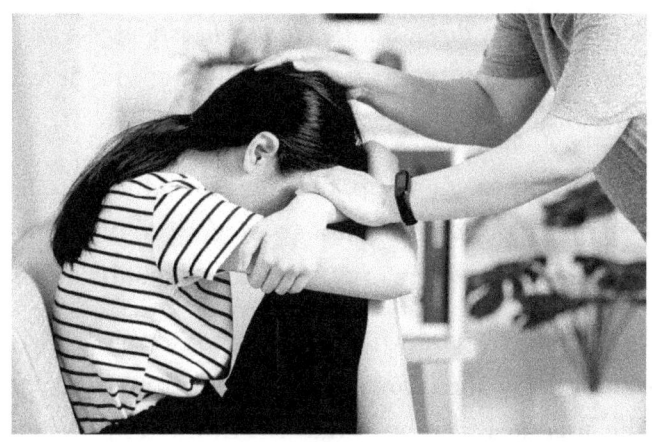

THE STORY OF TOO MANY

One of our academy students walked through the door after what seemed like just another school day. But as tears welled up in her eyes and she broke down in front of her mother, it became painfully clear—something was terribly wrong.

This little girl was once a ray of sunshine—always smiling, always laughing. But over the past few weeks, her mother watched with growing concern as that light began to fade. The joyful, energetic child she knew was slowly becoming quiet, distant, and withdrawn.

On this especially difficult day, her daughter seemed completely broken. Mom quietly hugged her, comforted her, and held her close. Then after some gentle encouragement and reassurance, the painful truth came out—she had been suffering in silence for months.

At school, a classmate had been tormenting her day after day—whispering cruel insults, poking her in the back, snatching things from her hands, and flooding her with hurtful words. The words cut the deepest: *ugly, dirty, dumb. No one likes you. No one wants to be your friend.* The bullying was unrelenting, and it was slowly breaking her down.

She was too afraid to speak up, fearing that telling the teacher or anyone else might only make things worse. Even more heartbreaking, she began to believe the cruel words and insults hurled at her.

Mom was devastated. Until now, bullying had felt like something distant—something she'd only heard about from other parents or seen in the media. But now it had hit home, and her own child was suffering.

That heartbreak quickly turned into determination. She knew she couldn't stay on the sidelines—she needed to understand, take action, and be part of the movement to stop this crisis that so many kids and teens are facing every day.

OUR PURPOSE AND MISSION

This book grew out of that painful moment—and the countless others like it experienced by parents and teachers all too often.

Its purpose is simple, yet deeply important: *to provide comprehensive, clear, and actionable guidance to help parents and educators understand, prevent, and break the cycle of bullying.*

Designed specifically as a guide for parents and teachers, it aims to empower the key adults in children's lives with the knowledge and tools needed to make a meaningful and lasting impact.

This guide will provide vital information to support parents and educators, including:

- Clear definitions, common misconceptions, and insight into the bullying cycle
- Recommended strategies for resolving conflicts effectively
- Tools to help children and teens build confidence and reduce their risk of becoming victims
- Practical ways to foster confidence, kindness, compassion, and empathy—helping prevent bullying before it starts

This guide brings together research, recommendations, and strategies from trusted sources such as the Centers for Disease Control and Prevention (CDC), the National Institutes of Health (NIH), and leading national and international bullying prevention initiatives. In addition to expert recommendations, you'll find real-life examples, practical tools, and supportive resources tailored to help you address bullying in your specific context.

Whether you're a parent navigating bullying in your child's school or social life, a mentor, coach, or teacher working to foster a safe and respectful classroom environment, this guide is designed to be a trusted reference—offering clarity, guidance, and hope in the effort to prevent and resolve bullying in every environment.

DEFINING BULLYING AND THE IMPORTANCE OF THIS GUIDE

First, let's define what bullying is and what it *is not*.

> *Bullying is generally described as a repeated, intentional behavior that aims to harm, intimidate, or coerce someone perceived as vulnerable.*

Bullying can take many forms—physical, verbal, social, and, increasingly, digital.

Unlike isolated incidents of conflict or disagreement, bullying is systematic, repeated, and involves an imbalance of power.

According to the *American Psychological Association*, bullying leads to severe emotional and psychological harm, affecting both victims and perpetrators.

The importance of addressing bullying cannot be overstated. Consider these alarming statistics:

- One in five students reports being bullied.
- The effects of bullying can be devastating, leading to anxiety, depression, and even suicidal thoughts.
- According to the *National Center for Education Statistics*, children who are bullied are more likely to experience academic struggles and social isolation.

These statistics underscore the importance and urgency of our mission and why it's imperative parents, teachers and community work together.

Throughout this guide, we will explore several key aspects of bullying, including:

- **The psychology of bullies and victims** - understanding the root causes of these behaviors.
- **Practical strategies for intervention** - learning when and how to step in.
- **Building empathy, compassion, confidence, and resilience** in children - developing skills to help prevent and support resolution for those affected.
- **Cyberbullying** - a growing form of harassment, will receive special attention, providing you with tools to protect children in the digital age.
- **Parent-teacher collaboration** - its importance and how a united front can make a significant impact on the well-being of children.

This book's structure is designed to guide you through these complex issues step-by-step. Each chapter focuses on a specific aspect of bullying.

- The first chapter **defines bullying** and **dispels common myths.**
- The next chapters explore the **psychology behind bullying** behavior and the significant **influence of adults** in children's lives.
- The following chapters offer practical strategies for **developing a strong foundation of confidence** in

children, **prevention and intervention strategies,** explore the challenges of **cyberbullying,** and provide guidance on **creating safe, supportive environments** for children and teens.

- **Personal stories and accounts** shared throughout the guide help to inspire and bring key concepts to life.
- Finally, a wide range of **references and resources** are provided for parents and teachers seeking additional guidance and assistance.

The vision for this guide is to go beyond definitions and statistics, serving as a beacon of hope and a practical resource. It aims to equip you with the knowledge and skills to help prevent bullying, recognize its signs, intervene effectively, and create environments where empathy and respect will thrive.

ABOUT THE MASTER METHOD ACADEMY

Since 2011, The Master Method Academy's education and outreach programs have made profound contributions to local, national, and international communities, working with students, public and private schools, organizations, and businesses.

The academy's mission is to deliver positive education, instill self-confidence and self-esteem, and promote thriving, healthy lives in mind, body, and spirit. Its programs emphasize cultivating a positive mindset, enhancing mental and physical health, preventing bullying, and safeguarding children.

Programs and initiatives include confidence development, leadership training, martial arts, success education, and community outreach—serving communities at every level, from local to global.

The academy's team is a diverse coalition of certified educators, school administrators, educational psychologists, wellness and life coaches, mental health professionals, parenting experts, mentors, and business and community leaders. The team also includes world champion athletes, martial arts grandmasters, and Olympians, blending a spectrum of unparalleled expertise with decades of experience.

Leveraging extensive research and the latest respected resources, The Master Method Academy addresses bullying from multiple angles. In addition to referencing current data and respected information, its team draws on years of experience working with thousands of students, parents, teachers, and school administrators to provide practical, comprehensive strategies and recommendations.

We now invite you to join us on this important journey. As you engage with the content, apply the strategies, and take meaningful action, you become a vital part of the healing, prevention, and lasting change our children need. Together, we can end the cycle of bullying and build a world where every child feels safe, valued, and respected. Your involvement is crucial—and with the right tools, knowledge, and compassion, you can make a powerful difference in both the present and future of our children.

Let's get started!

GETTING STARTED
HOW TO USE THIS GUIDE EFFECTIVELY

This comprehensive reference guide is designed to be a practical, easy to navigate resource for parents, teachers, mentors, and all adults who support children.

Whether you're addressing an urgent bullying concern—such as supporting your own child who has been targeted—or you're an educator working to implement prevention strategies to create a safer environment for children, this guide offers recommendations, insights, and tools drawn from trusted organizations and the latest research.

For parents in particular, you'll find actionable steps for prevention strategies, responding to your child's needs with empathy and confidence, rebuilding their sense of safety, and working with schools to ensure a consistent, supportive response.

Designed to be flexible and easy to navigate, the following tips will help you get the most out of the valuable information:

- **Read it cover to cover** to gain the most comprehensive understanding of bullying dynamics, recommended prevention strategies, and long-term solutions.
- **Use the descriptive Table of Contents** to jump directly to the topics most relevant to your needs—each chapter builds on the last, but they are also self-contained with practical, actionable guidance.
- **Explore real-life examples and case studies** to see how strategies have been successfully applied in everyday situations at school, home, and in the community. Use them as sources of inspiration to guide your own approach and adapt the ideas to fit your unique situation.
- **Put the tools, exercises, and conversation starters into practice** at home, in classrooms, or in community youth programs to help build confidence, empathy, and resilience in children.
- **Consult the resource list at the end** for hotlines, advocacy groups, and professional support when additional guidance or intervention is needed.

This is more than an informational reference—it's a trusted companion designed to help you protect, guide, and empower the children who need you most.

CHAPTER 1
UNDERSTANDING BULLYING
A CLOSER LOOK AT WHAT BULLYING IS, THE TYPES, AND WHY IT HAPPENS

SUFFERING IN SILENCE

During a routine parent-teacher conference, a concerned father shared his worries about his son Jack's sudden shift in behavior. Once a curious and enthusiastic learner, Jack had grown anxious, withdrawn, and was now frequently pretending to be sick just to avoid going to school.

The root of his distress? Relentless bullying.

After several gentle but persistent attempts to get him to talk, Jack's dad finally convinced him to open up. Tearfully, Jack began to share the traumatic experiences he had been keeping inside. Nearly every day at recess, a group of three boys from his class would corner him. The leader was a tall popular kid with two "side-kicks," and they would mockingly call him "Mini-Me" because of his small size, shove him as they walked past, and laugh when he fell in the dirt. They made fun of his lisp, called him "homeless" because his clothes were faded hand-me-downs, and cruelly nicknamed him "Scarface" because of a small scar above his eye. He had started hiding in the bathroom during lunch and recess—just to avoid being seen.

Jack went on to describe the torment on the school bus, where those same kids threw trash at him and whispered insults about his worn-out clothes and "ugly face" loud enough for him to hear. He was terrified to walk home alone, always taking the long way through the neighborhood to avoid known trouble spots. His heart pounded with every step. The fear followed him into the evening, keeping him awake at night, and he dreaded each new morning.

Even worse, he was too afraid to tell anyone. He thought that speaking up would only make the bullying worse. He felt completely alone.

His father, heartbroken and shaken, felt helpless. He had no idea it had gotten this bad. Desperately, he reached out to the school, hoping they would take action and offer support, guidance, and solutions before more damage was done.

Stories like this reveal a heartbreaking reality: far too many children endure bullying in silence and feel alone. That's why it's more important than ever to deepen our understanding of bullying, challenge common myths and misconceptions, and take thoughtful, informed action to protect children and help break the cycle for good.

1.1 BULLYING - WHAT IT IS AND WHAT IT ISN'T

The term *"bullying"* is often misunderstood or misused; therefore, having a clear and accurate definition is essential for recognizing it and responding appropriately.

According to the *Centers for Disease Control and Prevention (CDC)*: **Bullying involves unwanted aggressive behavior that is repeated over time and includes a power differential between the perpetrator and the victim.**

Most definitions of bullying highlight three key elements: repeated aggressive behavior, the intent to cause harm, and an imbalance of power.

These three elements distinguish bullying from other forms of conflict.

- **Repeated aggressive behavior** means that the actions occur multiple times over a period of time, rather than being isolated incidents.
- The **intent to harm** suggests that actions are purposeful, aimed at causing physical, emotional, or psychological pain.

- The **power imbalance** can be physical, social, or psychological, making it difficult for the victim to defend themselves.

In addition to defining what bullying is, it is important to address common misconceptions and understand what it is *not*.

- A common myth is that *"bullying is just a part of growing up."* This belief downplays and minimizes the serious and lasting impact bullying can have on a child's well-being.
- Another common misconception is the phrase *"boys will be boys,"* which often excuses aggressive behavior as a natural part of their development, while overlooking the real harm it causes.
- The idea that *"bullying is only physical"* is also a myth. Bullying can also be verbal, social, and now increasingly, digital. *The American Psychological Association* stresses that bullying can manifest through words or subtle actions, not just physical contact.

Leading organizations such as the *CDC (Centers for Disease Control and Prevention), UNESCO (United Nations Educational, Scientific and Cultural Organization),* and the *APA (American Psychological Association)* provide well-researched definitions and key insights into the nature and impacts of bullying.

- The *CDC* defines bullying as "unwanted aggressive behavior by another youth or group of youths involving a power imbalance and repeated actions."
- *UNESCO* highlights that bullying "is a global issue, emphasizing the need for healthy, safe learning environments."

- The *APA* adds that bullying "includes intentional and repeated behavior designed to cause injury or discomfort, whether through physical contact, words, or subtle actions."

These definitions highlight the complex nature of bullying and the need for a deeper understanding to address it effectively.

Bullying has been perceived and handled differently across cultures and throughout history. In the past, it was often dismissed as a rite of passage—a way to toughen up young people. Today, we understand the lasting harm it can cause and take it far more seriously.

Cultural perspectives also play a role in how bullying is perceived and dealt with. In some cultures, certain aggressive behaviors might be normalized or overlooked, while in others, there is a strong emphasis on communal harmony and respect, which leads to more social accountability.

As awareness has grown, anti-bullying policies have evolved to reflect a deeper commitment to student well-being. Today's policies are more comprehensive, often including prevention, intervention, and resources that promote safer, more inclusive environments for all students.

Understanding the true definition of bullying is the first step in addressing it effectively. When we recognize the key elements—repeated aggressive behavior, intent to cause harm, and an imbalance of power—we can clearly distinguish bullying from other types of conflict.

Clearing up common misconceptions helps us better identify what bullying is *not*, so we can recognize it more accurately, and respond in ways that are informed and appropriate.

Expert insights remind us that bullying is a complex and evolving issue. As the world changes, so do the ways children experience and respond to it. When we understand the full picture, we're better prepared to take effective and meaningful action and to protect the children who need us most.

1.2 THE FOUR SHADOWS OF BULLYING: PHYSICAL, VERBAL, SOCIAL, DIGITAL

Four Types of Bullying

Bullying appears in several forms, each with distinct signs and effects. Understanding these different types is essential to recognizing the problem and responding most effectively.

- **Physical bullying** - Often the easiest to recognize, physical bullying involves hitting, kicking, pushing, or other forms of physical harm meant to intimidate or hurt the victim. Picture a child coming home with unexplained bruises or torn clothing. These can be the first indicators of this type of bullying. But the damage goes far beyond what we can see. Victims of physical bullying often live in a constant state of fear, which can severely affect their mental health, emotional well-being, and ability to focus or succeed in school.
- **Verbal bullying** - Though less visible, verbal bullying can be just as harmful. It includes name-calling, insults, teasing, and other forms of verbal abuse. A child

experiencing this type of bullying may be targeted with cruel remarks about their appearance, intelligence, or abilities. Over time, the steady stream of negative words can leave lasting emotional scars, chipping away at their self-esteem, and leading to deep, long-term emotional trauma. For instance, a child repeatedly called "stupid" or "ugly" may begin to internalize those labels, believing them, and carrying that weight into their mental and emotional well-being.

- **Social bullying** - Also known as *relational bullying*, it involves behaviors like spreading rumors, intentionally excluding someone, or damaging a person's reputation and friendships. This form of bullying is especially harmful because it attacks what children value most— their social connections. A child facing social bullying might suddenly find themselves eating alone at lunch or being left out of group activities without any clear reason, and the emotional toll can be severe. Social bullying erodes a child's sense of belonging and can lead to deep feelings of loneliness, anxiety, and depression. Imagine a student consistently left out of birthday parties or group projects—over time, this repeated rejection can create a lasting sense of isolation and unworthiness.

- **Digital or Cyberbullying** - The most recent and rapidly growing form of bullying, cyberbullying takes place through digital platforms like social media, text messages, email, and online forums. What makes it especially harmful is its constant presence—it can follow victims home, making the harassment feel inescapable. Cyberbullying may include sending threatening messages, posting cruel or embarrassing content, or creating fake profiles to humiliate or target someone. The anonymity of the internet often gives bullies the confidence to act more aggressively than they would in person, and the emotional impact can be intense. Victims may experience severe anxiety, depression, and a sense of helplessness, especially when the bullying is public or ongoing. For instance, a student who receives hateful messages or has private photos shared online may live in a state of constant fear and humiliation, even in what should be the safety of their own home.

Signs & Symptoms of Bullying

Recognizing and understanding the signs and symptoms of each type of bullying is key to timely and appropriate action and intervention.

- *Physical bullying* often leaves visible evidence—bruises, scratches, or other unexplained injuries. Parents and teachers should be especially alert if a child seems hesitant or unwilling to explain how these marks occurred.
- *Verbal and Social bullying* may show up in more subtle ways, such as a child suddenly withdrawing from friends, avoiding group activities, or seeming anxious when talking about social situations. These behavioral shifts can signal deeper emotional pain.
- *Digital / Cyberbullying* can be harder to spot, but certain behavioral changes may offer clues. A child who suddenly loses interest in their devices, becomes unusually secretive about their online activity, or appears upset after being online may be experiencing digital harassment.

Personal Stories

Personal accounts and real stories bring the realities of bullying into sharper focus.

- **Noah was a quiet, curious seven-year-old who faced daily torment from a group of boys in his class.** He once loved going to school, raised his hand enthusiastically, and asked endless questions. That all changed when a group of athletic "popular" boys targeted him for his academic enthusiasm. They called him "teacher's pet" and said he looked like a bug-eyed bookworm with his thick glasses. They shoved him in the hallway, yanked his backpack off of him and kicked it down stairways, scattering the contents while other kids laughed, and he carefully hid bruises from being punched and elbowed when they thought no one was watching. Eventually, Noah began stalling at the breakfast table, tying his shoes very slowly before getting to school, and dreading the moment he'd have to walk through the doors. He stopped raising his hand in class, started eating lunch in a secluded corner, and did everything he could to shrink into the background everywhere he went. What hurt most wasn't just the physical abuse—it was the silence of the bystanders, the missed glances from teachers, and the feelings of isolation and belief that no one would step in. Instead of feeling safe and supported in a place he used to enjoy, he felt fearful, alone and hopeless.
- **Emily, a sixth-grade girl, was verbally harassed day after day by a tough girl and her friends who sat behind her in math class.** The tough girl was the ring leader, she made fun of Emily's weight, whispering cruel nicknames

like "whale" and "chubs," just loud enough for Emily to hear, and her followers in the back of the class would giggle and chime in as well. They laughed when she raised her hand to ask a question or gave a wrong answer in class. They called her "special" and "dumb" for not knowing the answers. What started as occasional teasing became daily relentless torment, and soon, even students who once spoke to her either joined in, laughed nervously, or simply looked the other way. The words didn't leave visible bruises, but they hurt deeply. Emily stopped speaking up in class, avoided group activities, and began eating lunch alone in the bathroom. Her once bright spirit dimmed, she became quiet and withdrawn, and her grades plummeted as she struggled to focus or care about school. Her teachers noticed the change but didn't realize the full extent of what she was enduring.

- **Jenna was a high school sophomore whose experience with social bullying left her isolated and heartbroken.** It began subtly, when friends she once laughed with at lunch and spent time with outside of school began sitting elsewhere at lunch, ignoring her texts, and leaving her out of weekend plans. Then came the rumors, whispers behind her back, and lies about things she supposedly said. Innocent comments were twisted to make her seem cruel or fake, and one by one, classmates distanced themselves. Soon Jenna found herself completely cut off from the social circles where she once felt part of and welcome. She began eating lunch alone in the courtyard, pretending to scroll through her phone just to avoid eye contact with anyone passing by. Group projects became a source of dread. The rejection and negativity stung deeply, not just because she lost friendships, but because it made her question her own worth. The loneliness was overwhelming, and walking the school halls felt like a minefield of stares, whispers, and cold shoulders. Despite showing up each day, Jenna felt more invisible than ever.

- **Fifteen year old Daniel became the target of relentless cyberbullying.** It started with a few cruel comments on one of his Instagram posts—remarks about his "gothic" appearance and making fun of his hair style, taste in music and questioning his political views. But things escalated quickly. Anonymous accounts began flooding his profile with hateful messages, calling him names, questioning his worth, and even encouraging him to harm himself. Someone at school found an old, awkward photo and shared it in a group chat, where it was edited into a cruel meme and reposted across multiple platforms. Within days, Daniel became the subject of online ridicule, and his notifications became a constant stream of digital cruelty. Unlike traditional bullying, the harassment followed him into every personal space including his bedroom, his weekends, and his quiet moments. There was no refuge, no break from the onslaught, and it was taking a severe toll on Daniel emotionally. He was once an outgoing student who enjoyed gaming and photography, but now he was withdrawing from friends, skipping school, and spending hours alone in his room. The anxiety and humiliation eventually turned into depression, and he began to lose hope that things would ever get better.

These stories are just a few examples of what so many young people face today. Each form of bullying—whether physical, verbal, social, or digital—leaves a deep and lasting impact.

Understanding how bullying shows up, recognizing the signs, and knowing how to respond are essential steps in breaking the cycle.

By staying aware, informed, and actively engaged, parents and educators play a vital role in quickly recognizing the signs of bullying making it possible to step in early, offer support, and help keep children and teens safe.

1.3 THE BULLY, THE BULLIED, AND THE BYSTANDER: ROLES & DYNAMICS

The bullying cycle refers to the ongoing loop of harmful behavior where the bully gains power through repeated actions, the victim is continually targeted, and bystanders either contribute to or passively allow the behavior to continue. This cycle can escalate over time if not interrupted, becoming deeply ingrained in school or social environments.

Understanding the bullying cycle is key to breaking it. It is not just about isolated incidents between a bully and a victim—it's a repeated pattern of behavior reinforced by roles and reactions.

Each role—the bully, the bullied, and the bystander—brings its own characteristics and behaviors, and each contributes to the overall dynamics of the cycle.

- **The Bully** - Bullies are often driven by a need for power and control. This need can stem from various factors, including a challenging home environment or a lack of empathy and social skills. They may display aggressive behavior to assert dominance and may often have been victims of bullying themselves. They may exhibit traits such as impulsivity, a lack of remorse, and a tendency to shift blame onto others. Often, they choose victims they believe they can overpower, reinforcing their need for dominance and control.

- **The Bullied** - Bullied victims tend to exhibit characteristics that make them more vulnerable to targeting. They might have low self-esteem, lack confidence, appear socially isolated, or have fewer friends. These children often respond to bullying with withdrawal, anxiety, or visible behaviors that may be uncharacteristic.
- **The Bystander** - Someone who witnesses the actions and interactions of the bully and the bullied can play a passive or active role. Passive bystanders do nothing, often out of fear of becoming targets themselves. In contrast, active bystanders may intervene to stop the bullying or actively support the bully by encouraging the bully's negative behaviors.

Psychological Impacts

Each role within the bullying cycle comes with its own mental and emotional challenges, all of which can shape a child's well-being over time.

- **The Bully** - While bullies may seem confident or in control, their behavior often stems from deeper emotional struggles such as insecurity, anger, low self-esteem, or a desire for attention and validation. These unresolved issues can fuel their aggression and trap them in a difficult cycle that's challenging to break.
- **The Bullied** - Those who are bullied often suffer serious emotional consequences, including chronic anxiety,

depression, and in severe cases, suicidal thoughts. Their academic performance may decline, and they may withdraw socially, feeling isolated and unsafe both at school and beyond.

- **The Bystander** - Witnesses to bullying can also experience psychological distress. Passive bystanders may struggle with guilt, helplessness, or regret for not stepping in, while active bystanders may feel anxious about retaliation or becoming targets themselves.

Beyond the emotional toll on those directly involved, bullying has a far-reaching impact that touches the entire school community. The way bullies, the bullied, and bystanders interact plays a major role in keeping the cycle going, and those effects extend well beyond the individuals at the center.

Power dynamics often drive this cycle. Bullies seek control, victims are left feeling powerless, and when bystanders remain silent—even if they don't agree with what's happening—that silence can be seen as approval. This lack of intervention can indirectly encourage the bully, allowing the behavior to continue or even escalate.

Over time, the damage spreads. Classrooms grow tense, students begin to feel unsafe, and trust between peers starts to erode. What may begin as isolated incidents becomes a school-wide issue with a ripple effect that can impact learning, relationships, and overall well-being.

That's why understanding each role in the bullying cycle is so important. Change doesn't happen by addressing only one part. We must work together, understanding every factor, while also zooming out to the bigger picture as a whole, in order to shift the dynamic. Every student, teacher, and caregiver has a part to play in breaking the cycle and building a school or community culture rooted in respect, safety, and inclusion.

Strategies for Intervention

To truly support everyone involved, intervention strategies must be tailored specifically to each role in the bullying cycle to be effective.

- **Reform the Bully** - Changing a bully's behavior requires targeted interventions that address the root causes of their actions and involving responsible caretakers and significant adults to help hold them accountable. Programs that teach empathy, emotional regulation, and social skills—such as anger management and conflict resolution—can lead to meaningful change. Empathy training, in particular, helps bullies understand the real impact of their actions on others, fostering accountability and growth.
- **Support the Bullied** - Helping those who have been bullied starts with emotional support and opportunities for healing. Counseling, peer support, and safe spaces to share their experiences can make a significant difference. Schools can offer support groups where students feel heard, understood, and guided by both peers and professionals. These efforts help rebuild confidence, self-worth, and emotional resilience. Including influential adults and caretakers in supporting the healing process outside of the school environment is also vital to this effort.

- **Empower the Bystander** - Empowering students to become "upstanders," to speak up, or safely step in can shift the dynamic dramatically. Schools can offer training that teaches students how to recognize bullying, intervene appropriately, and report incidents to trusted adults. Creating a culture where speaking up is encouraged, supported, and rewarded can help break the silence and promote a safer, more connected school community.

Each role—the bully, the bullied, and the bystander—has a unique influence on the bullying cycle. Understanding these roles and their psychological impacts is key to effective intervention.

A well-rounded approach that reforms the bully, supports the bullied, and empowers the bystander is essential for breaking the cycle and building a culture rooted in respect, safety, and inclusion in and out of school.

1.4 THE PSYCHOLOGY OF BULLYING: ROLES & MINDSETS

To effectively address and break the cycle of bullying, it's essential to understand the distinct psychological traits, mindsets, motivations, and challenges associated with each role—the bully, the bullied, and the bystander.

The Bully

Understanding the mindset of a bully involves exploring both psychological traits and environmental influences.

- One key driver is a **desire for power and control.**

- Bullies often **seek to dominate others** as a way to cope with their own **insecurities or a lack of control** in other areas of their lives.
- The **need to assert superiority** can show up in aggressive, intimidating behavior.
- The **home environment** plays a significant role as well. Children raised in homes where aggression, hostility, or emotional neglect are common may learn to replicate those behaviors, believing that dominance and intimidation are acceptable ways to interact.
- Additionally, a **lack of empathy** and **poor social skills** often contribute to bullying behavior. Many bullies struggle to recognize or care about the feelings of others, which makes it easier for them to cause harm without guilt.
- Lack of emotional awareness may stem from **inadequate support and guidance at home during important stages of their development.**

The Bullied

On the other side of the bullying dynamic are the targets—children who often possess certain vulnerabilities that make them more susceptible.

- **Low self-esteem and a lack of confidence** are common traits among those who are bullied. These children may already feel inferior or disconnected, making them easy targets for those seeking control. In some cases, this sense of inferiority begins at home, where parents may unintentionally undermine a child's self-worth with words of criticism, belittling or a lack of praise.

- **Social isolation** adds another layer of vulnerability. Without strong friendships or a support network, a child is less likely to stand up for themselves or report what's happening. The absence of allies can intensify feelings of helplessness.
- **Past trauma** can also increase a child's risk. Children who have experienced abuse, loss, or other emotional hardships may be more emotionally fragile, leaving them less equipped to handle bullying and more likely to internalize the hurt.

Together, these psychological and environmental factors create conditions that can make certain children more likely to be targeted.

The Bystander

Often overlooked, bystanders play a powerful role in the bullying dynamic. Whether they act or remain silent can significantly influence whether the bullying continues.

- One of the biggest reasons bystanders don't intervene is **fear**—especially fear of becoming the next target. This fear of retaliation keeps many students from speaking up, even when they know what's happening is wrong.
- Another key factor is the **diffusion of responsibility**— the belief that someone else will step in.
- In group settings, this mindset often leads to collective silence, a phenomenon known as the **bystander effect.**
- However, bystanders also have the **potential to become powerful allies.** When they feel empathy toward the victim

and a strong sense of moral responsibility, they are more likely to take action—whether by intervening directly, offering support to the victim, or alerting a trusted adult.

The Science Behind Bullying

To ground our understanding of bullying in science, we turn to established psychological theories and recent research.

- Albert Bandura's *Social Learning Theory* suggests that **behavior is learned by observing and imitating others** —especially when those behaviors appear to be rewarded. In the context of bullying, children may adopt aggressive behaviors after witnessing them in their environment, particularly when those behaviors go unpunished or are reinforced by attention or approval.
- The *Olweus Bullying Prevention Program,* a well-established, research-based initiative, emphasizes the **importance of addressing the environment** in which bullying occurs. It promotes the **creation of a school culture where bullying is clearly unacceptable and where positive, respectful interactions are consistently encouraged, rewarded, and reinforced.**

Recent studies on empathy and aggression strengthen this understanding, revealing important conclusions.

- **Fostering empathy in children at home and in school can lead to a significant decrease in aggressive behavior** and a boost in prosocial actions like kindness and cooperation.

- As a result, **empathy training** has become an essential element of effective anti-bullying programs.

When we understand what drives bullying behavior, why certain children are more vulnerable, and what holds bystanders back from stepping in, we begin to see the bigger picture.

Breaking the bullying cycle requires targeted strategies and a supportive environment where every child feels safe, seen, and empowered.

This foundation of understanding lays the groundwork for the strategies and solutions presented in the chapters ahead—each focusing on fostering safer, more caring spaces for children.

1.5 SUBTLE BULLYING: EXCLUSION AND ONLINE HARASSMENT

Subtle bullying is harder to detect than overt acts of physical or verbal aggression, and it often includes social exclusion and online harassment. Unlike physical bullying, subtle forms often leave no visible scars—but the emotional wounds can run deep.

- **Social exclusion** involves intentionally isolating someone from their peer group, whether by leaving them out of social events, spreading rumors to damage their reputation, or giving them the silent treatment. Though less visible, these actions can be just as hurtful and damaging as physical or verbal bullying.
- **Online harassment,** a common form of subtle bullying, takes advantage of the anonymity and wide reach of digital platforms. It can include posting hurtful

comments, sharing embarrassing photos, or creating fake profiles to spread lies and rumors.

Both social exclusion and cyberbullying are especially damaging because they often invade spaces that should feel safe—like a child's home—making the effects even more overwhelming and difficult to escape.

Impacts of Subtle Bullying

The impacts of the subtle bullying of social exclusion or online harassment are both serious and lasting.

Social exclusion can lead to long-term psychological effects.

- Children who are consistently left out may begin to internalize the rejection, developing deep feelings of self-doubt and a diminished sense of value.
- Ongoing isolation can severely affect their confidence and social development, leading to depression, chronic loneliness, and low self-worth.

Online harassment results in other layers of harm.

- The relentless and often anonymous nature of digital bullying can cause intense anxiety and emotional distress.
- Victims may live in constant fear of the next attack, which can lead to sleep problems, trouble concentrating, physical symptoms like headaches or stomachaches, and a noticeable drop in academic performance.

- For young people still forming their identity and self-esteem, the emotional toll of being targeted online can be devastating and difficult to recover from.

Recognizing Subtle Bullying

Subtle bullying can be harder to detect than physical bullying, but the signs are often present in a child's behavior.

In **social exclusion,** a child may be deliberately isolated by peers. Some key behavioral indicators include:

- Withdrawal from social activities
- Avoiding eye contact
- Becoming unusually quiet or anxious

In cases of **online harassment**, changes in digital behavior can be telling:

- A child becomes secretive about their device use
- Frequently checks their phone with visible distress
- Suddenly loses interest in social media
- Parents and educators should monitor and observe for negative online interactions, such as harsh comments, suspicious messages, or altered communication patterns.
- Encouraging open dialogue about digital experiences can help reveal issues early.

Responding to Subtle Bullying

Addressing subtle bullying effectively requires a multi-layered approach.

Important factors and recommendations for parents and educators to consider:

- **Foster Open Communication**
  - Create a safe, judgment-free space for children to share (*Example: Let your child know they can talk to you about anything—good or bad—without fear of getting in trouble. When they do share, actively listen, validate their feelings, and support them.*)
  - Ask open-ended questions regularly (*Example: Instead of "Did you have a good day?", ask "What was the best part or hardest part of your day?" to encourage deeper conversation. Ask follow-up questions and how they felt in situations they are sharing about.*)
  - Listen actively and validate their feelings (*Example: When a child says, "I felt left out at recess," respond with, "That sounds really hard—I'm glad you told me. Can you tell me more about what happened?"*)
- **Build School-Based Support Systems**
  - Implement peer mentoring programs to foster connection and belonging (*Example: Pair older students with younger ones for weekly check-ins, helping them feel seen, supported, and included in school life.*)
  - Encourage group work and inclusive classroom activities (*Example: Rotate group assignments so students collaborate with different classmates, breaking down cliques and encouraging new friendships.*)
  - Promote kindness, empathy, and mutual respect in daily interactions (*Example: Begin the day with a class gratitude circle or recognition shout-outs to highlight kind acts and positive behaviors.*)

- **Strengthen Digital Safety**
  - Create Structured Rules, Boundaries, and Close Monitoring of Digital and Online Activity (*Example: Set up classroom or household tech agreements outlining expected and appropriate device use, screen time limits, and consequences for violations.*)
  - Establish Clear, Accessible Reporting Mechanisms for Online Issues (*Example: Provide an anonymous online form or dropbox in classrooms or counselor's office where students can safely report cyberbullying or digital concerns.*)
  - Make Sure Students Know How to Report Inappropriate Behavior and Feel Safe Doing So (*Example: Regularly remind students at home, in classes or during assemblies how and where to report digital issues, and reinforce that their concerns will be taken seriously and confidentially.*)
  - Offer Digital Safety Workshops to Teach Respectful Online Behavior, Privacy Awareness, and Cyberbullying Prevention/Resolution Strategies
  - (*Example: Partner with local law enforcement or digital citizenship organizations to host workshops, seminars, or interactive sessions on managing digital footprints and responding to online harassment.*)

Recognizing and Responding to Subtle Bullying - Case Examples

- **Case 1: Social Exclusion in Middle School** - Once included in group chats and weekend plans with other boys in his neighborhood, Brian was now routinely ignored, left out of planned get-togethers, and spent lunch periods sitting alone in the far corner of the cafeteria, picking at his food in silence. He had always been a happy, energetic student, but over the course of a few months, his spark had faded. He stopped participating in class, his grades were dropping, and he became noticeably withdrawn. Thankfully, his homeroom teacher, Ms. Rodriguez, and his mother noticed the changes in Brian and began checking in with him more frequently. After several gentle, open-ended conversations, Brian finally shared how invisible and alone he felt at school. His mom contacted the school counselor, who had already spoken with Ms. Rodriguez. They invited Brian into their peer mentoring program, pairing him with two supportive eighth-grade students, Ben and Christopher. They met weekly, offered encouragement and invited him to join special interest clubs and group activities. Over time, Brian's confidence grew, he smiled more, participated in class again, and began forming real friendships in and out of school.

- **Case 2: Cyberbullying in High School** - Seventeen-year-old Jessie became the target of relentless anonymous online harassment during the fall of her junior year. After innocently posting a fun beach photo with a boy she was friends with, cruel and insulting messages began flooding her social media. Comments made fun of her weight, criticized her outfit, and even worse, spread false rumors about her relationship with the boy. Manipulated images with humiliating captions were created and quickly shared across multiple accounts, reaching what felt like the entire school within hours. The online world, once a space of connection and creativity for Jessie, suddenly became a source of fear and anxiety. She stopped posting, avoided her phone, retreated to her room at home, and became quiet and withdrawn at school. Her parents noticed the change. Through gentle and persistent inquiries, they encouraged her to open up, and she finally tearfully shared what had been happening. With their support, she reported the harassment. The school acted quickly and connected Jessie with Ms. Atkins, a trusted counselor, and digital safety lessons and policies were implemented to raise awareness about cyberbullying and respectful online behavior. Over time, things began to settle. With continued encouragement from her family and school, Jessie started to re-engage socially and rebuild her confidence with strategies in place to protect her digital space. She knew she wasn't alone, and that asking for help had truly made all the difference.

Subtle bullying, such as social exclusion and online harassment, can have serious emotional consequences, but with the right approach, it can be effectively addressed.

A few recommended strategies:

- **Recognize the warning signs early and take immediate action to prevent long-term harm.** Early intervention can stop bullying behaviors before they escalate and cause deeper emotional trauma.
- **Foster open communication and reassurance so children feel safe sharing their experiences.** When children know they'll be heard without judgment, they are more likely to speak up and seek help. Encourage dialogue with students and create opportunities to share their feelings on various topics, so it becomes a comfortable practice.

- **Establish strong support systems in schools to ensure no child feels isolated.** Trusted relationships with teachers, counselors, and peers provide a vital safety net for those affected. Established systems and a structure of support will provide a proactive response to help students in need more effectively.

When parents and educators stay vigilant and take proactive steps quickly and consistently, the benefits are far-reaching:

- **Children feel safer and more supported.** A sense of security builds confidence and allows students to focus on learning and personal growth.
- **School communities become more inclusive and emotionally healthy.** Supportive environments help all students thrive academically, socially, and emotionally.
- **A culture of empathy, respect, and accountability begins to take root.** These values, once modeled and reinforced at home and at school, shape a child's behavior both in and out of the classroom.

Together, these efforts do more than just break the bullying cycle —they help build a lasting culture of safety, respect, and belonging, where each child's voice matters and their well-being is a priority.

CHAPTER 2
THE POWER OF ADULTS
DEVELOPING KNOWLEDGE AND SKILLS TO ADDRESS BULLYING & PROVIDING MEANINGFUL SUPPORT TO CHILDREN

THEY'RE ALWAYS WATCHING

When eight-year-old Jordan got into trouble for mocking his classmate Robby's stutter during a group reading activity, Ms. Williams was not only surprised, she was sad and disappointed. Jordan was usually so kind and helpful and the type of student who offered to sharpen pencils or walk a classmate to the nurse. However, recently she had noticed subtle changes in him—

sarcastic remarks under his breath, exaggerated eye-rolls, and quick laughs at others' mistakes.

When she called his mother to discuss what had happened, the pieces started falling into place. "Oh, we joke like that all the time at home," his mother said casually. "Especially now that he's getting older. You've got to toughen kids up. They can't be so sensitive." The teacher suddenly understood: Jordan wasn't being intentionally cruel, he was repeating what he saw and heard. The teasing, the dismissive tone, the belittling humor—it was all learned behaviors. Like so many children, Jordan had been paying close attention to the adults in his life, absorbing, mimicking, and reflecting their behaviors back into the world around him.

Every word, action, and reaction from an adult leaves an imprint on a child's view of the world. How we speak to and about others, how we respond to conflict, or how we treat people who are different—our choices as adults become their blueprint. If they hear kindness, they learn kindness. If they see respect, they practice respect. But when sarcasm, bias, or indifference are modeled, children mirror those too.

This chapter reveals how parents, teachers, mentors, and even strangers shape the way young people learn to interact, show empathy, demonstrate courage, and treat others. The example adults set can either fuel or help break the cycle of bullying.

2.1 THE ROLE OF ADULTS: WHERE BULLYING PREVENTION BEGINS

Adults have a profound influence on the way children develop behaviorally and socially, including how they understand and respond to bullying. Studies have consistently shown that **chil-**

dren learn by observing and imitating the behaviors and attitudes of the adults in their lives. This underscores the importance of parents, teachers, and caregivers modeling behaviors that promote empathy, kindness, respect, confidence, and inclusion.

When adults consistently demonstrate these values, they send a clear message about what is acceptable and expected. Their actions shape not only how children see themselves, but also how they treat others. In this way, **positive behavior modeling** becomes a powerful tool in bullying prevention—laying the foundation for a safe, respectful, and inclusive environment where all children can feel valued and secure.

2.2 BEHAVIOR MODELING: WHAT WE WANT CHILDREN TO LEARN

Behavioral modeling shows that individuals—especially children—learn by observing and imitating the actions of others.

- Albert Bandura's influential work on **social learning theory** (1977) emphasizes that children are especially likely to replicate behaviors they observe in adults, especially those they view as authority figures or role models. This social learning is an active process.
- Children don't just mimic behavior—**they internalize what they observe, and as a result, their own beliefs, emotional responses, and social behaviors are shaped.**

Modeling isn't only about avoiding negative behaviors—it's about **intentionally demonstrating the positive actions and behaviors we want children to learn.**

- When adults consistently show kindness, empathy, and respectful communication, they offer children real-life examples of how to interact in healthy, constructive ways.
- In contrast, when adults model or tolerate negative behaviors like yelling, name-calling, criticism, gossip, or exclusion, they send an unspoken message that these actions are acceptable.

Remember, what we model matters—because children are always watching, learning, and reflecting what they see.

2.3 THE HOME ENVIRONMENT: PARENT INFLUENCE ON CHILDREN'S BEHAVIORS

The home is often the first environment where children learn social behaviors.

- Parental influence is profound, as parents are typically the most significant figures in a child's early life.
- Children observe how their parents interact with others, handle conflicts, and manage emotions, and they tend to replicate these behaviors in their interactions with others, especially peers.

One of the most influential positive behaviors parents can model is empathy. **Empathy is the ability to understand the feelings of another--putting yourself in their shoes,** and it's a foundational skill that can help prevent bullying.

- When parents demonstrate empathy in their daily interactions—whether by listening attentively to others, showing compassion in difficult situations, or discussing emotions calmly and openly—they teach their children to value and practice empathy themselves (Eisenberg & Strayer, 1990).

Parents who model respectful, peaceful communication and healthy conflict resolution provide their children with essential tools to navigate social challenges without resorting to negative behaviors that could lead to bullying.

- For example, parents who calmly discuss and resolve disagreements rather than shouting or using hurtful words demonstrate to their children that conflicts can be resolved constructively.
- This modeling helps children understand that negativity or aggression is not a necessary or effective response to conflict.
- In contrast, children who witness or experience aggressive or disrespectful behavior at home are more likely to exhibit similar behaviors in their interactions with peers.
- Studies have shown that **children who grow up in environments where aggression is normalized are at a higher risk of perpetrating the bullying cycle,** either as an aggressor or a victim (Holt et al., 2009).

2.4 THE SCHOOL ENVIRONMENT: TEACHERS AND SCHOOL STAFF INFLUENCE

Teachers play a pivotal role in shaping the social atmosphere of their classrooms and the attitudes of the children they teach.

The behaviors that teachers model are observed closely by students and often set the standard for acceptable behavior in and out of the classroom. Therefore, teachers have a unique opportunity and significant responsibility to **model behaviors that discourage bullying, conflict, and negativity and to promote a positive, peaceful, and inclusive environment.**

- **Fostering an inclusive classroom environment** where all students feel valued and respected is one of the most effective ways teachers can prevent bullying. Modeling inclusivity by acknowledging and celebrating the diverse backgrounds and abilities of their students sends a powerful message about the importance of acceptance and respect. For instance, a teacher might incorporate diverse cultural awareness into the curriculum, allowing students to share their traditions and cultures with classmates. This not only broadens students' understanding of the world but also fosters an environment of mutual respect and curiosity about differences, rather than fear or exclusion.

- **Preventively setting clear expectations from the outset that bullying will not be tolerated is as important as addressing bullying when it occurs.** Teachers can do this by establishing a clear classroom code of conduct at the beginning of the school year, co-created with students, that emphasizes respect, kindness, and inclusion. For example, a teacher might facilitate a discussion on what it means to be a good classmate, guiding students to collectively agree on behaviors that promote a positive classroom culture.

- **Immediately, actively, and consistently intervene in bullying situations or in addressing any behaviors not**

in keeping with a kind and positive culture. This prompt and proactive approach demonstrates that negativity is unacceptable and will not be tolerated. It also further reinforces the expectations of a culture of respect and safety for students (Olweus, 1993).

- When bullying does occur in the school environment, teachers should **intervene immediately, separating the students involved and addressing the behavior in a way that is firm yet respectful.** For instance, rather than simply punishing the bully, a teacher might use the situation as a teaching moment, helping the student understand the impact of their actions and guiding them toward more empathetic behavior. This could involve restorative practices, such as having the student who bullied others make amends through a face-to-face apology or by participating in activities that promote empathy and understanding.

- Teachers can **model conflict resolution skills and mediate discussions** between students who have disagreements. Helping them to see each other's perspectives and find common ground can not only help resolve the immediate conflict but also equip students with tools to handle future disagreements in a non-physical, constructive manner.

- **Integrate social-emotional learning (SEL) into the** daily routine, which can help build a foundation of empathy, self-awareness, and social skills among students. Activities such as group reflections, peer mentoring, and role-playing scenarios can be powerful ways to teach students how to navigate social situations positively. For example, a teacher might lead a role-play exercise where students practice responding to exclusion or teasing in ways that defuse tension and promote understanding.

- **Publicly and positively acknowledging students who stand up against bullying** with assertiveness and respect, helps reinforce a culture of safety and respect. For example, if a student reports bullying or steps in to support a peer, a teacher can commend that behavior in front of the class, while still protecting the privacy of those involved. This kind of recognition sends a clear message: courage, empathy, and standing up for others are valued. It validates the student's actions and encourages others to follow their lead, fostering a classroom environment where bullying is not accepted by peers—and where kindness and accountability are the norm.

2.5 SARCASM: ITS EFFECTS ON CHILDREN

Consistency is key when it comes to modeling positive behavior, especially for parents or adults in leadership roles like teachers, coaches or other role models. Children carefully observe adult behavior and often mimic what they see. When a parent or teacher discourages name-calling but uses sarcasm or belittling comments, it sends mixed messages that can undermine the goal of creating a safe, respectful environment.

Sarcasm, in particular, can be especially harmful and **should be avoided in any environment, but especially in school and home settings.**

- Younger children often interpret sarcastic remarks literally.

- Older children may misread the tone or intent.
- What might seem like a harmless joke to an adult can feel confusing, hurtful, or even shaming to a child.
- Over time, these mixed signals can erode trust and contribute to an environment where children feel uncomfortable, uncertain, insecure, or devalued.
- Children who are regularly exposed to sarcasm may imitate it without understanding its subtleties. This can lead to inappropriate or hurtful interactions, further disrupting classroom harmony or in settings outside of school.
- **Research has shown that sarcastic or belittling comments from adults can negatively affect a child's self-esteem, increase anxiety, and interfere with their ability to form healthy social relationships (American Psychological Association, 2017).**

To prevent these negative outcomes:

- Adults should strive to **use clear, supportive, and respectful language** that aligns with the behaviors they hope to see in children. For example, instead of using sarcasm to point out a mistake, a parent or teacher might say, "It looks like there was a mix-up—let's figure it out together." This not only leads to resolutions and correcting behaviors, but it also reinforces relationships and develops a culture of empathy and growth.
- By being **intentional and thoughtful with words and actions**, adults can foster a safe and inclusive environment where children feel respected, valued, and supported.

A mindful approach of avoiding sarcasm and consistently modeling positive behaviors strengthens relationships at home, builds classrooms rooted in trust and encouragement, and promotes healthy interactions—all of which will help prevent and discourage behaviors that contribute to the bullying cycle.

2.6 OTHER ADULT INFLUENCES: COACHES, COMMUNITY & THE MEDIA

While parents and teachers are the primary adult influences in a child's life, other adults—such as coaches, community leaders, and even media figures—also play a significant role in shaping a child's social behavior. These broader influences can either reinforce or undermine the lessons children learn from their parents and teachers.

- **Community leaders and mentors**, for example, can provide powerful examples of leadership and respect. When these figures model positive behavior, such as showing fairness, advocating for others, or demonstrating resilience in the face of challenges, they help children understand the importance of these values in real-world contexts.
- Similarly, **the media** plays a significant role in modeling behavior for children, often serving as a source of social norms and expectations. Unfortunately, the media can also expose children to negative behaviors, such as aggression, exclusion, or superficiality, which can contribute to the normalization of bullying.
- When children are exposed to **negative modeling**— whether in their communities, schools, or media—adults must actively counteract these influences. Sometimes it

may be necessary to remove the influence. It can also be addressed by discussing the negative behaviors observed, explaining why they are harmful, and offering positive alternatives to those behaviors.

It is crucial for parents and other adults to proactively guide children, closely monitoring their exposure to outside influences, limiting or removing it if necessary, and critically evaluating negative behaviors they observe.

2.7 PRACTICAL STRATEGIES: MODELING POSITIVE BEHAVIOR

Modeling positive behavior requires intention and awareness. Adults must be conscious of the behaviors they display in front of children and take advantage of opportunities to demonstrate the values they want children to adopt.

- One of the most effective strategies is to model **everyday kindness and respect.** This can be as simple as using polite language, offering help to others, or showing appreciation for someone's efforts. Children who regularly observe such behaviors are more likely to incorporate them into their own social interactions.
- Strive to model positive behavior **consistently across different settings**—whether at home, at school, or in public spaces. Consistency helps reinforce the message that these behaviors are not situational but are fundamental aspects of one's character.
- Modeling **apologies and accountability** teaches children to acknowledge their own mistakes and take responsibility, helping to develop honesty and integrity. It

helps children understand that making mistakes is part of being human, it's important to acknowledge them, and what matters most is how we respond and make amends.

- Adults can **model emotional regulation** and emotional intelligence by managing their own emotions in healthy ways. Taking deep breaths when stressed, expressing feelings calmly, and seeking constructive solutions to emotional challenges are all healthy strategies children can learn through observation of the adults in their lives who practice them consistently. Learning to understand and manage their own emotions in healthy ways will reduce the likelihood of emotional outbursts that can lead to negative behaviors.

2.8 CHALLENGES: RECOGNIZING, OVERCOMING & BREAKING THE CYCLE

Modeling positive behavior is not without its challenges. Adults, like children, are influenced by their own experiences, stressors, and environments, which can sometimes lead to lapses in behavior.

Recognizing these challenges and working to overcome them is essential for positive behavior modeling.

- **Self-awareness and reflection** are critical first steps. Adults must be willing to examine their own behaviors and attitudes, identifying areas where they may need to improve. This can be challenging, especially if it involves confronting long-standing habits or beliefs. However, it is a necessary step in ensuring that the behaviors we model align with the values we wish to instill in children.

- **Breaking the cycle** of negative behavior is another challenge that many adults face, particularly those who may have experienced or modeled negative behaviors in the past. This can be addressed through education, support, and a commitment to change.
- By **seeking out resources**, such as parenting classes, therapy, or peer support groups, adults can develop the skills and strategies needed to model positive behavior effectively.
- **Parents, teachers, and other community members must work together** to reinforce positive behavior modeling. This can be achieved through open communication, shared goals, and mutual support. By working together and supporting each other, adults can create a consistent and supportive environment for children, making it easier to model the behaviors that will prevent bullying.

2.9 SUCCESS STORIES: EFFECTIVE POSITIVE BEHAVIOR MODELING

Success stories from families and schools that have implemented effective modeling strategies provide valuable insights into the power of this approach.

- Studies have shown schools and families focused on empathy-building exercises and consistent positive behavior modeling by adults observe significant reduction in bullying behaviors. Children report feeling safer and more supported, and an overall school climate and home environment is improved.

Challenges, struggles, and finding solutions also offer important lessons.

- In other examples, parents struggling with managing their own anger and finding support through parenting programs learn techniques for emotional regulation. By modeling these strategies at home, they not only improve their own behavior but also observe positive changes in their children's interactions with peers—including a noticeable reduction in aggressive behavior.

These examples illustrate that while modeling positive behavior can be challenging, it is both achievable and effective when approached with intention and proper support.

2.10 LONG-TERM IMPACTS: ADULT BEHAVIOR RIPPLE EFFECTS

In this chapter, we've explored the profound influence adult behavior has on children and how these influences can play an important role in preventing bullying. The way adults model respect, empathy, and kindness sets the tone for how children interact with one another.

Teachers, parents, and other role models have the power to create environments that promote understanding and discourage harmful behaviors. This chapter has highlighted practical strategies for modeling positive behavior, underscoring the need for consistency and mindfulness in our interactions with children.

The behaviors adults demonstrate today don't just impact the current generation—they lay the foundation and create positive long term effects for a more empathetic and respectful society.

When children observe adults handling conflicts with calm grace, showing empathy toward others, and responding to negativity with positivity, they learn to replicate those behaviors. This ripple effect can help foster a culture of kindness and confidence, where respect and inclusion are the norms, and ultimately leading to a future where bullying is diminished.

2.11 CALL TO ACTION: WE EACH PLAY A ROLE

The responsibility to model positive behavior extends beyond just parents and teachers; it is a collective duty of all adults who interact with children. By consciously embodying values of respect, empathy, and understanding, we can help shape a world where bullying has no place.

Each of us plays a critical role in this effort, and through consistent, thoughtful behavior, we can inspire a new generation to treat others with dignity, respect, and positivity.

CHAPTER 3
CONFIDENCE DEVELOPMENT
A KEY TO HELP CHILDREN FEEL WORTHY AND CAPABLE, NO MATTER WHAT OTHERS SAY OR DO

WHY CONFIDENCE MATTERS

Confidence is more than just a personality trait—it's a powerful form of protection. **Children who carry themselves with confidence in their posture, voice, communication, and actions are far less likely to be targeted by bullies.** Bullies often single out those they perceive as vulnerable, isolated, or unlikely to speak up for themselves, so confidence development helps tremendously in preventing these situations. This principle applies to adults as well —confidence can shape how others perceive and respond to us in personal, professional, and social situations.

While no child (or adult) is ever at fault for being targeted, **building strong self-confidence can reduce the risk of being victimized and provide the tools and inner strength to face challenges.**

It's important to be clear: no one is ever at fault for being bullied. But building strong self-confidence can serve as a powerful protective factor, helping to prevent being targeted, and to feel more empowered and better equipped to handle difficult situations if they arise.

It's important to **begin nurturing confidence early in childhood.** When children develop a strong sense of self from a young age, they're more likely to stand up for themselves, resist negative peer pressure, make healthy choices, persevere, and navigate challenges as they grow into teens and adults.

This chapter offers practical, research-based strategies and exercises to help parents and educators help develop lasting confidence in children—empowering them from the inside out.

3.1. BODY LANGUAGE: PROJECTING CONFIDENCE NON-VERBALLY

Confident body language communicates strength and self-assurance without saying a word. Children can learn to hold their heads high, stand tall, maintain appropriate eye contact, and use calm, purposeful movements to project confidence and discourage bullying behaviors.

Strategies and Exercises:

- **Power Poses:** Have children practice standing tall with shoulders back, feet firmly planted, and heads held high. Research shows that adopting "power poses" for even a few minutes can boost feelings of confidence.
- **Mirror Practice:** Let children practice eye contact and assertive facial expressions in the mirror. Praise their efforts and help them see the difference between "shy" and "confident" posture.
- **Role-Play Situations:** Practice walking into a room confidently, greeting others, or responding to teasing using assertive body language.
- **Real-Life Practice:** Give children frequent opportunities to practice building confidence in everyday situations. Encourage them to order their own food at a restaurant, ask a store employee for help, or pay at a register. These small moments help them practice speaking clearly, making eye contact, and interacting with others in real-world settings—skills that will strengthen, develop, and become more natural and comfortable over time.

Tip for Parents and Teachers: Gently encourage confident body language such as standing tall, shoulders back, eye contact, and even smiling during practice and real-life sessions. The more they practice, the more it will become natural, and eventually reminders won't be necessary.

3.2. VOICE AND TONE: COMMUNICATING WITH CONFIDENCE

The way a child uses their voice can significantly impact how they are perceived and how effectively they can express themselves. Teaching children to speak clearly, use a calm but firm tone, and project their voice appropriately helps them feel more in control and assertive. Practicing volume control, expressive speech, and respectful language empowers children to communicate confidently while maintaining kindness and respect.

Strategies and Exercises:

- **Volume Awareness:** Help children understand appropriate voice levels for different settings, including speaking up when necessary and lowering their voice when needed.
- **Tone Practice:** Use scenarios to explore how tone can change the meaning of a message. Practice saying the same sentence in different tones and discuss the impact.
- **Clear and Calm Responses:** Teach children to pause, take a breath, and speak in a calm, clear voice, especially in situations involving conflict or teasing.
- **Role-Playing Scenarios:** Practice assertive phrases like "Please stop," or "That's not okay," using a firm but respectful tone. Reinforce that assertiveness doesn't mean being rude.
- **Encourage Expression:** Promote expressive speaking by reading aloud or storytelling. Emphasize clarity, projection, and emotional expression to help them find their voice.

Tip for Parents and Teachers: Praise children when they use their voice effectively and respectfully. Point out moments when their confident voice made a difference in a positive interaction.

3.3 ASSERTIVENESS VS. AGGRESSION: CONFIDENCE WITH KINDNESS

Confidence isn't about being loud, combative, or trying to dominate others. One of the most valuable lessons we can teach children is the difference between being assertive and aggressive.

Assertive means standing up for oneself in a clear, respectful, and confident way, and expressing thoughts, needs, or boundaries without violating the rights of others. In contrast, being **aggressive** often involves hostile, forceful or loud negative behavior that can escalate conflict or cause harm.

Teaching children to be assertive—not aggressive or passive— empowers them to advocate for themselves while still treating others with kindness and respect.

Strategies and Exercises:

- **"I" Statements:** Teach children to express themselves with calm, clear "I" statements. Example: "I don't like it when you say that. Please stop." Avoid "you" statements which can sound confrontational and make others defensive. Example: "You always do that. You're mean."
- **Boundary-Setting Scripts:** Develop and rehearse scripts children can use when someone crosses a boundary. Practicing these responses in advance—through role-play or guided conversation—can help children feel more

prepared and less anxious in the moment. Reinforce the idea that it's okay to speak up, set limits, and remove themselves from situations where they feel unsafe or disrespected.

Examples:

> *"That wasn't very nice. Can you please stop that."*
> *"I don't like that—please stop,"*
> *"I don't think that's funny. Let's talk about something else."*

- **Tone of Voice Practice:** Help children recognize the difference between a timid, aggressive, and assertive tone. Use games to identify and practice different tones in a safe space. Practice "I" statements using an assertive confident tone, versus an angry confrontational tone.

Tip: Praise children not just for speaking up, but for doing so with kindness, clarity, and assertiveness.

3.4 SOCIAL CONFIDENCE: BUILDING CONNECTIONS

Loneliness and social isolation are major risk factors for becoming a target of bullying. Helping children develop friendships and social confidence creates a safety net and reinforces self-worth.

Strategies and Exercises:

- **Playdate Planning and Group Activities:** Encourage participation in clubs, sports, or interest-based groups where kids can form connections naturally with children who have similar interests and values.

- **Teach Conversation Starters:** Practice simple conversation openers children can use with peers. Compliments are a great way to start positive interactions.

Examples:

> "I heard you're really good at soccer—could you teach me sometime?"
> "I like your shirt—where did you get it?"
> "Your hair looks so cool!"

- **Compliment Challenges:** Create a family or classroom challenge to give genuine compliments each day. This promotes kindness and teaches kids how to look for the good in people and initiate positive interactions.

Tip: Model positive inclusive behavior to children by treating others with kindness and respect. Introduce your child to others, while encouraging welcoming positivity, curiosity, and empathy in social settings.

3.5 POSITIVE SELF-TALK: POWERFUL STRATEGIES TO BUILD INTERNAL CONFIDENCE

A child's internal dialogue has a powerful impact on how they see themselves. Developing positive self-talk can become a strong defense against self-doubt and becoming a target of bullying.

Strategies and Exercises:

- **Success & Gratitude Journals:** Encourage children to keep a journal where they write down things they did well that day, something they are grateful for, or other positive moments or experiences from their day. It's okay if they repeat entries, especially if they are similar accomplishments from previous days. The important thing is this simple habit of daily reflection helps shift their focus from self-criticism to self-recognition and gratitude, which helps to build confidence and develop a strong, positive mindset.

- **Affirmations:** Create daily affirmation routines that children can easily practice each day. Writing affirmations is especially powerful—whether in their success journal, on cards, or on sticky notes placed around their room, these visible reminders help reinforce positive self-beliefs. Phrases like "I am strong," "I am smart," and "I believe in myself" can build self-confidence and resilience over time. Regular repetition of affirmations helps reframe their inner dialogue and strengthens their sense of self-worth.

- **Become a Thought Detective:** Teach children to challenge negative thoughts by asking questions like: "Is this *really* true?" "Is this thought helpful to me?" and "What's a more positive way to look at this?" Encourage them to imagine their best friend or someone they love having the same thought. What would they say to support them? This simple exercise helps children think more critically about their self-talk, guiding them to replace limiting beliefs with more empowering and positive thoughts.

Tip: Reinforce that it's okay to feel nervous or scared—those feelings are normal. Remind children that courage isn't the absence of fear; it's about choosing to act in spite of it. Sometimes, just **20 seconds of bravery**—whether it's raising their hand, speaking up, or introducing themselves—those 20 seconds can lead to meaningful growth, pride, and a big boost in confidence.

3.6 EMPOWERMENT: INVOLVING CHILDREN IN GOAL-SETTING AND DECISION-MAKING

When children feel a sense of control in certain areas of their lives, their confidence naturally grows. Giving them age-appropriate responsibilities and involving them in everyday decisions fosters independence, builds self-confidence, and strengthens their inner strength.

Strategies and Exercises:

- **Choice-Making Opportunities:** Allow children to make age-appropriate decisions, such as choosing what to wear, which game to play, or how to spend their free time. This builds decision-making skills and helps children feel a sense of control and autonomy in their daily lives.
- **Weekly Goal Setting:** Encourage children to set one small, personal goal each week (e.g., "I will ask one classmate to play at recess") and celebrate their progress. Goal-setting promotes motivation, builds self-discipline, and reinforces a growth mindset.
- **Family or Class "Leadership Roles":** Assign rotating roles that give children a chance to lead and take responsibility, such as being the line leader, helping with meal planning, or managing classroom tasks. Leadership

roles foster responsibility, boost confidence, and give children a sense of purpose and contribution.

Tip: Praise effort, not just outcomes. Emphasizing growth, progress, and the willingness to try new things (even when it feels scary), helps children develop a growth mindset. This encourages resilience, perseverance, and a healthy attitude toward learning and challenges.

EXERCISE: Journal Entry - Confidence Building

Create a list of daily or weekly activities designed to build confidence and self-esteem. This visual tool can serve as a tangible guide for children to follow, helping them stay focused on their self-esteem building journey.

Examples:

- Write three positive affirmations. Reflect on each one as it is written. Close your eyes, and create a picture in your mind of what that affirmation looks like.
- Set a small goal. List the steps you need to take to reach the goal. Make a daily checklist of tasks you need to do each day to get you closer to the goal.

Developing confidence and self-esteem is a multifaceted process that involves

- **understanding** its importance
- **actively engaging** in specific activities
- leveraging **mentorship and role models,** and
- addressing **common challenges**

By focusing on these areas, you can help children build the confidence they need to prevent or face bullying issues and thrive in social situations.

CONFIDENCE AS A PREVENTIVE TOOL

Confidence is not about perfection. It's about belief in one's worth, voice, and ability to face and conquer challenges with courage. As parents and educators, we can instill this belief early on by creating environments and opportunities where children feel supported, acknowledged, and capable. With confident body language, assertive communication, social skills, positive self-talk, and decision-making practice, children can develop the inner strength, resilience, and positive mindset needed to not only stand strong in the face of bullying, but to rise above it.

CHAPTER 4
EMPATHY & RESILIENCE
HELPING KIDS OVERCOME BULLYING WITH CONFIDENCE, AWARENESS, AND MENTAL SELF-DEFENSE STRATEGIES

When one of our academy parents attended her daughter's third-grade open house, the teacher pulled her aside with tears in her eyes. "Your daughter has a gift," the teacher said. "Today, another student had a meltdown, and your daughter sat quietly beside him, handed him a tissue, and said, 'It's okay. I've had days like that too.'" Mom smiled, humbled but not surprised. At home, their family always talked openly about feelings, read books about kindness, and intentionally modeled compassion during everyday moments. Her daughter wasn't just learning how to succeed—she was learning how to connect, comfort, and lead with compassion. Mom knew as she proactively taught and modeled this to her child that these were the qualities that would help her child through life's inevitable challenges.

In a world where children face growing emotional and social challenges, empathy and resilience are not just nice-to-have traits—they're essential. These qualities equip kids to form healthy relationships, navigate adversity, and become compassionate, confident individuals. This chapter explores how parents, educators, and caregivers can intentionally foster these traits, offering practical strategies to help children thrive both emotionally and socially. The journey starts with simple, everyday actions that build strong hearts and thoughtful minds.

4.1 EMPATHY BUILDING ACTIVITIES: TEACHING KIDS TO UNDERSTAND AND CARE

Empathy is the ability to understand and care about the feelings of another, by truly putting yourself in their shoes. Empathy doesn't just happen—it's a skill that grows with guidance, practice, and real-life experiences.

When children learn to recognize and care about others' feelings, they lay the groundwork for healthy relationships, strong character, and emotional resilience. The strategies below are designed to help parents and educators intentionally nurture empathy in everyday life through meaningful, age-appropriate experiences at home and at school.

Teaching Empathy to Children: Key Strategies for Home & School

- **Role-Playing Scenarios**
  - By acting out different situations, children can step into the shoes of others and see the world from their perspective.
  - Example: One child acts as a new student feeling left out while others think of inclusive actions.Helps children understand emotions like loneliness and kindness through experiential learning.
- **Stories with Moral Lessons**
  - Stories have a way of touching the heart and making complex concepts relatable.
  - Books like *Wonder* by R.J. Palacio explores themes of kindness, acceptance, and understanding.
  - Sample discussion questions to deepen learning:
    - "How do you think Auggie felt when others stared at him?"
    - "What could you do to make a new student feel welcome?"
- **Empathy Games and Exercises**
  - *Emotion Charades*: Children act out emotions without words to enhance emotional recognition.
  - *Empathy Display*: Kids draw, sculpt, or visually represent how someone might feel in a situation.
  - These activities make emotional learning interactive, creative, and fun.

- **Classroom Strategies**
  - *Group Discussions*: During these discussions, students can share their experiences and listen to others, building a sense of community and understanding..
  - *Buddy System*: Pairing students together encourages peer support and helps children develop deeper connections with their classmates.
  - These strategies promote both empathy and a supportive classroom environment.
- **Using Literature and Media**
  - Watching films or reading books as a class or family and discussing the characters' experiences can lead to meaningful conversations about empathy.
  - Films like *Inside Out* help children visualize and relate to complex emotions.
  - Books serve as windows into others' lives and experiences, making them a valuable tool to promote empathy.
- **Building Empathy at Home**
  - *Family Meetings*: Share daily highs and lows to encourage emotional expression and empathy.
  - *Kindness in Action*: Encourage small gestures like writing thank-you notes or helping siblings.
  - *Parental Modeling*: Demonstrate empathy in your own actions—children often learn by example.

EXERCISE: Journal Entry - Empathy

Previously, we recommended encouraging your child to keep a journal to write about successes, gratitude and other positive experiences. Guiding them each day to journal with various prompts gives them a valuable opportunity to reflect and express their feelings.

For their "EMPATHY" journal entry, ask them to think about interactions they've had with others recently.

- Describe an experience when they felt empathy for someone else or when someone showed empathy toward them.
- Reflect and journal about empathy on a regular basis, as often as possible.
- This practice helps children create empathetic awareness in themselves, in others, and it reinforces the importance of understanding and caring for others.

Empathy can be cultivated through simple, intentional moments woven into daily life. When children engage in role-playing, listen to stories, play empathy-based games, and share in open conversations, they begin to see the world through others' eyes. These everyday practices help them grow into thoughtful, caring individuals—and ultimately, help shape a kinder, more connected community.

4.2 RESILIENCE TRAINING: HELPING CHILDREN BOUNCE BACK FROM CHALLENGES

When we talk about **resilience**, we're referring to a child's ability to adapt, recover, and bounce back from adversity, stress, or trauma. It's what helps them keep going when life gets tough.

- **Emotional resilience** is the capacity to recognize, manage, and recover from emotional pain or difficult feelings. It allows children to face sadness, frustration, or disappointment without becoming overwhelmed.
- **Psychological resilience** involves mental strength and flexibility. It's the ability to think clearly, stay focused, and maintain a sense of hope when facing challenges, setbacks, or pressure.

Together, emotional and psychological resilience form a foundation that helps children handle life's ups and downs with confidence and courage.

Building Resilience in Children Facing Bullying

For children experiencing bullying, resilience is not just helpful—it's essential. It can mean the difference between feeling overwhelmed by emotional pain and rising stronger, confident, with a clear sense of identity and self-worth.

A few key strategies include:

- Helping children develop **problem-solving skills.** Encourage them to think through challenges and come up with their own solutions. For instance, if a child is being bullied, work with them to brainstorm options. This process builds confidence and reinforces their ability to take control of difficult situations. Guide them to understand and even role play the following strategies with you:

- *Ignore the bully.* Explain to them that sometimes, if you just walk away, it takes away their power and they no longer have someone to bother.
- *Compliment the bully.* A lot of times, the bully is not happy about him/herself. If they receive a compliment, it might help turn things around, and you might even gain a friend.
- *Tell a responsible adult.* If other strategies don't work, tell a parent, teacher, babysitter or other trusted adult. Explain that it's not "tattling," because by you telling them, it could help prevent it from happening to someone else.

- Learn and develop **coping strategies**. Simple techniques like breath work (e.g. slow deep intentional breaths in through the nose and out through the mouth), taking a break and counting to ten, or visualizing a peaceful place and resolutions can help children manage emotional stress in the moment. These small but powerful and intentional tools can make a big impact by helping them stay calm and grounded.
- Encourage **emotional regulation exercises**. Expressing feelings in their journal is a helpful strategy that can help children better understand their emotions and identify patterns in how they respond. With guided prompts to encourage expressing their thoughts and feelings, their journaling cultivates awareness and healthier choices, enabling them to bounce back more easily from setbacks.
- Seek out or develop programs that offer structured approaches to building resilience through strength-based and cognitive-behavioral strategies. These tools can be especially effective in school settings, where children can

practice resilience in a supervised and supportive environment.

Countless real-life examples show how resilience grows through connection, confidence-building activities, and proactive guidance and support. Some children who have experienced bullying find strength through sports, where teamwork and a sense of achievement help rebuild their self-esteem. Others discover support in peer groups that celebrate their individuality, allowing them to feel accepted and empowered.

Ultimately, resilience isn't something children are born with—it's a skill that can be cultivated and nurtured. With the right guidance, encouragement, and tools, every child can develop their inner strength to overcome, rise above bullying and thrive.

4.3 SOCIAL-EMOTIONAL LEARNING (SEL): INTEGRATING SEL INTO DAILY CURRICULUM

Social-Emotional Learning (SEL) is an educational approach that helps individuals—especially children—develop essential life skills such as empathy, emotional regulation, and responsible decision-making. These skills play a key role in fostering a supportive, inclusive environment where bullying is less likely to occur.

SEL helps children grow in **five fundamental areas:**

Self-awareness
Self-management
Social awareness
Relationship skills
Responsible decision-making

- **Self-awareness** involves recognizing one's emotions, thoughts, and values and understanding how they influence behavior. For instance, a child who understands their feelings of anger can better manage their reactions.
- **Self-management** is about regulating emotions, thoughts, and behaviors in different situations. It includes managing stress, controlling impulses, and setting personal goals.
- **Social awareness** is the ability to empathize with others from diverse backgrounds and cultures, understanding social and ethical norms for behavior, and recognizing family, school, and community resources.
- **Relationship skills** involve establishing and maintaining healthy and rewarding relationships based on cooperation, resistance to inappropriate social pressure, conflict resolution, and seeking or offering help when needed.
- **Responsible decision-making** is the ability to make ethical, constructive choices about personal and social behavior. It involves considering the well-being of oneself and others, recognizing the consequences of various actions, and evaluating the benefits and risks of different choices.

Several Social-Emotional Learning programs have proven effective in schools by helping students build essential life skills alongside academic growth.

- The **Second Step Program**, used from early learning through middle school, focuses on empathy, emotion management, problem-solving, friendship skills, and learning strategies. Its age-appropriate lessons build on each other year after year, reinforcing these skills over time.

- The **Collaborative for Academic, Social, and Emotional Learning (CASEL)** offers a widely used framework for integrating SEL at the classroom, school, and district levels. Their resources help schools embed SEL into daily instruction and school culture, making it a consistent part of students' educational experience.

SEL can also be integrated into daily school routines through simple activities.

- **Morning meetings** provide a space for students to express feelings and build empathy, setting a positive tone for the day and fostering a sense of community.
- **Group projects** encourage students to work together, solve problems, and support each other. These projects help develop relationship skills and social awareness, as students learn to navigate different perspectives and work towards common goals
- **Reflection journals** help students process emotions and learn from their experiences, develop self-awareness and responsible decision-making. Teachers can guide these reflections with prompts that encourage students to think about how they handle situations and what they might do differently next time.

The impact of Social-Emotional Learning programs in schools has shown to be extremely positive.

- Students show improved academic performance, better focus, and goal-setting abilities.

- Behavior improves as students learn to manage emotions and resolve conflicts.
- Most importantly, SEL supports mental and emotional well-being, helping children develop confidence, resilience, and equip them with life skills that extend beyond the classroom.

In addition to integrating Social-Emotional Learning into the school environment, SEL can be effectively incorporated at home through everyday parent and family interactions, with intentional practices that nurture a child's emotional intelligence and empathy qualities.

- Parents can model healthy behaviors and emotional expression by talking openly about their own feelings and calmly working through challenges.
- Creating daily routines that include moments for reflection—such as sharing highs and lows of the day during dinner or bedtime—can help children develop self-awareness, empathy, and peaceful problem solving skills.
- Encouraging peaceful problem-solving during conflicts, praising effort and kindness, and practicing active listening all reinforce SEL skills.
- Reading and discussing books together that explore emotions and social situations can also spark meaningful conversations.

By consistently integrating these simple yet powerful practices, families can build a supportive environment where children learn to understand themselves and relate positively to others.

Whether at school or at home, Social-Emotional Learning practices help children build stronger emotional well-being and thrive in all areas of life. By developing self-awareness, emotional regulation, empathy, and decision-making skills, SEL serves as a cornerstone of both well-rounded education and healthy child development.

4.4 ENCOURAGING POSITIVE BEHAVIOR: REINFORCING KINDNESS AND RESPECT

Positive Reinforcement

Encouraging positive behavior in and out of school through positive reinforcement is a powerful way to instill kindness and respect in children.

Positive reinforcement involves recognizing and rewarding desirable behavior to encourage its recurrence.

Techniques like verbal praise, tangible rewards, and special privileges can be highly effective. For instance, when a child shows kindness by helping someone, praising them immediately with specific feedback reinforces the behavior.

Reward systems—in school and at home–like sticker charts or points can inspire motivation for children to practice kind and respectful behavior. Initially, these incentives can reinforce and encourage positive actions and help establish consistency. However, the ultimate goal is to use these tools as stepping stones– as first steps to guiding children toward forming lasting habits. As healthy, positive behaviors become habitual, we would want them to shift to becoming a natural part of the child's character, practiced without the expectation of a reward, and that will come in time.

Creating a Positive Environment and Culture

Collective efforts and initiatives that promote kindness and respect as the norm all work together to create and nurture a positive environment and culture.

School-wide kindness campaigns can be a powerful tool. These campaigns might include activities like "Kindness Week" or "Kindness Challenges," encouraging students to perform kind acts regularly.

These initiatives can also be practiced at home with fun activities such as "Random Acts of Kindness" for family members, friends or neighbors. Examples: Cleaning up or helping with something around the house without being asked, doing yardwork for a neighbor as a surprise, or making a special card for a friend.

Practicing "Random Acts of Kindness" becomes part of the process to develop habits of kindness, empathy and respect to become part of their character.

Recognition and Acknowledgement

Celebrating acts of kindness during school assemblies, in classrooms, and in the home environment reinforces these values with positive recognition and sets a positive example, encouraging others to keep the energy going and perpetuating the positive culture.

Peer nomination and recognition programs allow students to acknowledge their classmates for kind actions, building a caring and supportive environment. A "Kindness Wall" can serve as a space to publicly recognize peers, visually reinforcing and praising positive behavior and strengthening the sense of community. At home, families can develop creative ways to encourage and acknowledge family members for their acts of kindness.

Community Involvement

Involving the community in encouraging and reinforcing positive behaviors extends the reach of Social-Emotional Learning beyond the classroom and home environment.

Involving youth in community service projects, like food drives or visits to nursing homes, gives them opportunities to practice kindness and develop social responsibility. These experiences deepen their understanding of empathy and meaningful contribution, and encourages focus and caring for others outside of themselves.

Collaborations with businesses, non-profits, and community groups can provide resources, sponsorships, and learning opportunities. These community relationships help reinforce kindness and respect and encourage positive interactions with a variety of people.

Integrating these strategies—positive reinforcement, a positive school and home environment, recognition/acknowledgement, and community involvement—helps create an environment where kindness and respect are not only encouraged but celebrated. This comprehensive approach benefits families, students, educators, and the broader community alike.

4.5 SELF-ESTEEM AND CONFIDENCE: DEVELOPING THE FOUNDATION TO FACE BULLIES

As we discussed previously, self-esteem, which encompasses self-worth and self-acceptance, forms the foundation of a child's self-confidence, and it plays a pivotal role in their ability to prevent or handle bullying situations.

When children possess a strong sense of self-worth, they are less likely to be affected by negative comments or actions from others. They understand their intrinsic value and are better equipped to assert themselves in social situations.

Confidence in social settings allows children to interact positively with their peers, making them less vulnerable to bullying. For, example, a child who believes in themselves and their worth is more likely to assertively say "no" to a bully, seek help when needed, and support others who might be targets.

To develop self-esteem and confidence in children, it's important to engage them in a spectrum of activities designed to reinforce their sense of worth, exposing them to as many positive experiences as possible to reinforce and amplify their effectiveness.

Just as physical development requires discipline and consistency in exercising muscles and physical abilities—mental, emotional, and confidence development requires consistent practice as well, and requires guidance, encouragement and coaching from supportive adults.

Some helpful confidence-building activites—some of which were mentioned earlier, but are worth repeating due to their lasting impact:

- **Affirmation exercises** encourage children to speak or write positive statements about themselves, such as "I am capable," "I am strong," or "I am worthy of respect." These affirmations, when repeated regularly, can help shift their mindset from self-doubt to self-assurance.
- **Goal-setting** activities and workshops guide children to set realistic, achievable goals and celebrate their progress. Achieving these goals, no matter how small, can significantly enhance their confidence.
- **Personal achievement entries in their journals** provides an opportunity for children to document their accomplishments and reflect on their growth. As we've mentioned before, by regularly writing down their successes, they can see tangible evidence of their abilities, reinforcing their self-worth.
- **Peer mentors** can play a significant role in helping to build self-esteem. Peer mentoring programs, where older students support younger ones, can foster a sense of relationship-building, belonging and confidence. These programs create a supportive environment where children can learn from their peers' experiences and challenges as well as diminishing feelings of loneliness.
- **Inspirational role models** who have overcome bullying and share their stories can inspire and give hope. Hearing firsthand accounts of resilience and triumph helps children realize that they, too, can overcome adversity. These role models serve as living proof that it is possible to rise above bullying and achieve great things.
- **Activities, sports or hobbies** designed specifically to build self-esteem and confidence can be fun and effective in helping in positive development and to become part of a community with positive values. Seeking the right fit for

your child and family is important, so it is important to ask for recommendations and do some research first.

Common self-esteem challenges and helpful strategies:

- **Fear of failure** is a significant hurdle for many children, and they may avoid trying new things or taking risks, which can prevent their growth and confidence-development. Explain to them that "not succeeding YET" does not mean "failure," and it's a natural part of learning. Sometimes it takes time, practice, and patience. This learning process allows you to grow and improve. Encourage a "growth" and "improvement" mindset, where mistakes are seen as stepping stones to success rather than setbacks. And success is in the learning, growing, and improving with each step taken.
- **Overcoming negative self-talk** is another critical challenge when children internalize negative comments from others, leading to a cycle of self-doubt. Help them recognize and challenge these negative thoughts. Encourage them to replace self-critical thoughts with positive, affirming ones. For example, if they think, "I can't do this," guide them to reframe it as, "I can learn how to do this." Sometimes pairing these conversations of encouragement and affirmations with calming breathing exercises will also help them to redirect, reframe and reset their thought patterns to more peaceful, positive thoughts of focusing on their goals, gratitude, and belief in themselves. This calming of the mind will help with motivation, inspiration, solutions, and progress.

EXERCISE: Journal Entry - Confidence Building

Create a list of daily or weekly activities designed to build confidence and self-esteem. This visual tool can serve as a tangible guide for children to follow, helping them stay focused on their self-esteem building journey.

Examples:

- Write three positive affirmations. Reflect on each one as it is written. Close your eyes, and create a picture in your mind of what that affirmation looks like.
- Set a small goal. List the steps you need to take to reach the goal. Make a daily checklist of tasks you need to do each day to get you closer to the goal.

Developing confidence and self-esteem is a multifaceted process that involves

- **understanding** its importance
- **actively engaging** in specific activities
- leveraging **mentorship and role models,** and
- addressing **common challenges**

By focusing on these areas, you can help children build the confidence they need to prevent or face bullying issues and thrive in social situations.

The next chapter will explore practical intervention strategies that parents and teachers can use to address bullying effectively and support both victims and bullies.

CHAPTER 5
INTERVENTION STRATEGIES
TAKING MEANINGFUL ACTION TO SUPPORT BULLIED CHILDREN WHEREVER IT OCCURS

Jake, a quiet high school freshman, had become an easy target for a group of older boys notorious for bullying underclassmen. They preyed on students who seemed timid or isolated—stealing money, supplies, and sometimes using physical force simply to intimidate. Their actions went unchecked for far too long, as most victims stayed silent, fearing retaliation.

One day, however, things took a different turn. While making his usual rounds, a sharp-eyed janitor noticed the group following Jake into the restroom. Something about the scene didn't sit right with him. Trusting his instincts, he followed—and stepped in just in time. He disrupted the harassment that was beginning to turn physical, de-escalated the situation and made sure Jake got out safely.

This janitor made it a point to do more than just clean the halls— he made it a priority to observe student behaviors and investigate anything that seemed off—believing that prevention is just as important as intervention.

Because of his vigilance and quick thinking, the school was finally made aware of what Jake—and likely others—had been enduring. Counselors and administrators stepped in to support Jake, and for the first time, he felt safe enough to speak up. They reassured him that speaking up about his experiences could help protect others and prevent similar situations in the future.

This story serves as a powerful reminder that immediate intervention matters. It not only protects a child in the moment—it prevents further harm to others, and it sends a clear message that bullying will not be tolerated. Adults must take every report seriously and act quickly to ensure the safety and well-being of every child. Every student deserves to feel safe, seen, and supported.

5.1 WHEN BULLYING HAPPENS: STEPS FOR IMMEDIATE RESPONSE

Immediate Action

If ever faced with a crisis, bullying situation or an incident needing adult intervention, acting swiftly is crucial to prevent further harm.

- **Immediately interrupting the interaction** should be your first step. Whether you're a parent witnessing an altercation at a park or a teacher observing bullying in the classroom, stepping in immediately can stop the situation from escalating.
- **Separate the involved parties** to ensure everyone's safety. This may mean directing them to different areas of the room or playground or physically placing yourself between the individuals.
- The primary goal is to **quickly and calmly address and de-escalate** the situation if necessary, and prevent any further physical or emotional harm.

Intervention Without Escalation

Intervening without escalating a tense situation requires a calm and composed approach.

- Speak in a **calm but firm voice** when addressing the children involved.

- **Avoid yelling** or using a harsh tone, as this can escalate tensions and resulting behaviors, making the situation worse.
- **State clearly and firmly** that the behavior is unacceptable and must stop immediately.
- **Avoid physical confrontation** at all costs. Physical intervention should only be used if absolutely necessary to ensure the safety of the parties involved, and should be used with extreme caution.
- **Focus on verbal commands** and positioning yourself in a way that creates a **physical barrier** between the individuals involved. This approach helps maintain control of the situation without adding to the chaos or fear.

Immediate Support

In bullying situations, once you have separated the involved parties, your attention should shift to immediately comforting and reassuring the bullied child.

- **Offer them a safe space** to talk about what happened. This could be a quiet corner of the classroom, a counselor's office, or any place where they feel secure.
- **Validate their feelings.** Let them know that their emotions are understood and that it is okay to feel upset, scared, or angry. Statements like, "I understand that this is very upsetting for you," can provide much-needed comfort.
- **Listen** to their account of the incident completely, without interruption or judgment, asking questions if

necessary to help them express themselves fully, and assure them that it is not their fault.

- This **immediate emotional support** can help alleviate trauma, helping them feel safe and supported.

Documentation

Immediately documenting the details of the incident ensures that you have an accurate account of what occurred, which is crucial for any follow-up actions.

Keeping detailed records helps create a clear timeline of events, which is essential for any interventions or disciplinary actions that may follow.

- Note the **who, what, when, and where** of the incident. Identify who was involved, what exactly happened, when it occurred, and where it took place.
- Collect **witness statements.** Witness accounts can provide additional perspectives and elaboration, which can help corroborate the victim's account.
- Ensure statements are collected from **multiple sources** to get a comprehensive view of the incident.

Documentation can be used to ensure accurate records are compiled and may be used to inform parents, school administrators, and, if necessary, law enforcement.

Preventing Further Harm and Future Incidents

When bullying or other crises occur, responding quickly and decisively can prevent escalation and lay the groundwork for a safe and supportive environment.

- **Interrupting** the behavior, calmly **separating** those involved, and **de-escalating** the situation are essential first steps.
- Offering **immediate support** to the victim helps them feel seen, heard, and reassured that they are not alone— and that their feelings are valid.
- **Careful documentation** of the incident ensures a clear, accurate record, which is vital for appropriate follow-up and accountability.

Response in these critical moments can make a lasting impact. Swift, compassionate action not only protects those directly involved but also sends a powerful message that bullying is never acceptable and will be taken seriously.

The steps you take in these critical moments lay the foundation for creating a safer, more supportive environment for all children.

5.2 SCRIPTS AND CONVERSATION STARTERS: TALKING TO CHILDREN ABOUT BULLYING

Open the Lines of Communication

Open communication is foundational in addressing bullying effectively. As a parent or teacher, creating a culture of communicating safely and having these conversations in a comfortable environment is crucial.

- Choose a time and place where the child feels safe and relaxed.
- In the classroom, a one-on-one discussion during a break or after school can provide the right setting.
- Quiet moments at home such as bedtime or in the car driving could be opportunities for open conversations and conducive to feeling comfortable sharing thoughts, feelings and experiences.
- The key is to ensure that the child feels they can speak freely without fear of judgment or interruption.
- Creating the best environment and opportunities to build trust will make it easier for the child to open up about their experiences and how they feel about them.

Scripts to Guide Conversations

Using effective scripts and talking points can be helpful in guiding important conversations when talking to children involved in the bullying cycle.

When talking to **the bullied** child:

- Start with empathy and understanding.
- You might say, "I've noticed you've seemed upset recently. Can you tell me what's been going on?"
- Asking questions with empathy opens the door for them to share their feelings.

If you're addressing **the bully:**

- It's important to remain calm and non-confrontational.
- A useful script might be, "I heard about what happened with [victim's name]. Can you help me understand what led to that?"
- Asking them to tell their story encourages the child to reflect on their actions without feeling attacked.

When engaging with **bystanders:**

- You could say, "I heard you saw what happened with [victim's name] and [bully's name]. Can you tell me how it made you feel? What do you think we can do to help?"
- Asking these questions allows them to share what they experienced, validates their feelings, but also involves them in finding a solution. Feeling involved in the resolution can help them feel empowered in breaking the bullying cycle and preventing it from happening to others.
- Asking these questions gives children a chance to share their experience, validates their feelings, and actively involves them in finding a solution. Being part of the resolution process can help them feel empowered, preventing it from happening to others.

Active listening

Using techniques to actively listen are essential for understanding the child's perspective when they are trying to express themselves.

- **Reflective listening,** where you repeat back what the child has said in your own words, shows that you are engaged and empathetic. For example, if a child says, "They always call me names during recess," you might respond, "It sounds like recess has been really tough for you because of the name-calling." This helps the child feel heard and understood.
- **Asking open-ended questions,** such as "Can you tell me more about how that made you feel?" encourages the child to share more details and express their emotions fully.
- **Avoid interrupting or offering solutions too quickly.** The goal is to understand their experience completely before moving forward with advice or possible solutions.

Ongoing Communication

Encouraging ongoing dialogue is vital for maintaining a supportive environment.

- Regular check-ins, such as weekly family meetings or classroom discussions, keep the lines of communication open.
- During weekly family meetings, everyone can share their highs and lows that week, providing a natural opportunity to discuss any issues that come up related to bullying.
- In the classroom, regular activities and discussions around social interactions, and safely expressing thoughts and feelings can normalize talking about emotions and experiences. The teacher's guidance and expectations for

these conversations will be important in creating a positive culture for this.

- Regular and ongoing guided conversations will help build a culture of openness, positivity, and support.

EXERCISE: Role-Playing Activity

Create a role-playing exercise where children can practice responding to bullying in different scenarios. This can be an activity for school or at home.

- One child/family member plays **the bully,** another **the victim,** and a third **the bystander.**
- Create different scenarios, giving each person a general description of how to behave and what to say in each scenario.
- After each scenario, discuss what happened, how it felt to each participant, and what could be said and done differently to improve the situation.
- After discussing examples of confident, kind and "upstanding" behaviors and responses, end the activity with one last positive and "best practice" scenario, with everyone practicing the best and recommended responses.

Examples:

- The Victim: Practice the strategies discussed previously such as—ignore the bully, compliment the bully, or tell a responsible adult.
- The Bystander: Practice phrases such as "That's not very nice, can you please stop that."

- This exercise helps children understand different perspectives and develop positive strategies for real-life situations.
- It gives them an opportunity to practice confident behaviors and responses, to feel more comfortable speaking up, and to develop confidence, kindness, compassion, and assertiveness.

Open, honest communication is one of the most powerful tools in addressing bullying. Using clear scripts, practicing active listening, and encouraging ongoing dialogue helps create a safe space where children feel comfortable sharing their thoughts and experiences.

When parents and teachers intentionally foster a supportive environment—one built on empathy, consistent check-ins, and meaningful conversations—children are more likely to speak up. This not only helps address bullying when it happens, but also builds a culture of trust that can prevent future incidents from occurring.

5.3 DOCUMENTING INCIDENTS: CREATING A PAPER TRAIL

When a child confides in you about a bullying incident, your immediate reaction might be to comfort them and ensure their safety. However, it's equally important to document and create a detailed record and timeline of the events to help establish patterns, identify recurring issues, and provide a concrete basis for interventions.

Documentation and creating a "paper trail" will be important when discussing incidents with school administrators, other parents, or even law enforcement if necessary. It serves as evidence that can substantiate claims and ensure that appropriate actions are taken.

To document bullying incidents effectively, follow a systematic approach.

- Start by using incident report forms, which can be provided by the school or created based on standardized templates.
- Report forms should include sections for detailing the incident, noting the date, time, and location.
- Maintain daily logs and journals where any observed or reported incidents are recorded.
- Consistent logging helps create a comprehensive picture of the bullying behavior, aiding in identifying patterns or escalation.
- Every entry should be concise yet detailed, capturing the essence of what occurred without ambiguity.

When documenting an incident, there are several important elements and details to consider.

- Begin with a clear description of the incident. Explain what happened in a factual manner, avoiding subjective language.
- Note who was involved, including the bully, the victim, and any bystanders.
- Witness statements are invaluable; they provide additional perspectives and can corroborate the victim's account. Collect these statements as soon as possible while the details are fresh in everyone's mind.

- Record the actions taken by you or any other adults present. Specify who intervened, what steps were taken to stop the bullying, and any immediate support provided to the victim.
- Including careful detail ensures that your documentation is thorough and reliable.
- Maintaining confidentiality is paramount when handling these sensitive records.
- Storing documents securely is essential to protect the privacy of all involved.
- Physical records should be kept in a locked cabinet, while digital records should be stored on secure, password-protected devices.
- When sharing information with others, be mindful of protecting the privacy of the children involved, complying with legal and ethical standards for handling or distributing personal information. Check with your school or local administrators for appropriate standards and protocols.

Thorough documentation is not just a bureaucratic exercise; it is a foundational step in addressing and resolving bullying. By creating clear, detailed records, you provide a solid basis for any interventions that may follow. This documentation helps ensure that the issue is taken seriously and addressed appropriately by all parties involved. It also provides a sense of security for the victim, knowing that their experience is being documented and taken seriously. Keeping these records secure and maintaining confidentiality respects the privacy of all children involved, fostering a trustworthy and supportive environment.

5.4 SETTING UP SAFE SPACES: CREATING INCLUSIVE ENVIRONMENTS

Creating a safe and inclusive environment for children involves both physical and emotional safety measures.

Physical safety starts with establishing safe zones within the child's environment. These areas are designed to be havens where students can retreat if they feel threatened or overwhelmed.

- Inside schools, designated "quiet rooms" provide a peaceful space for students to decompress and regain their composure. These rooms should be equipped with comfortable seating, calming decor, and resources like books or art supplies to help children relax.
- Similarly, safe zones outside on playgrounds ensure that even during recess, children have a place to go if they need to escape bullying or aggressive behavior. These zones should be supervised by adults who are trained to handle conflicts and provide support.
- Establishing safe zones at home can also allow children a place of refuge and peace. Establishing a quiet, comfortable space where they can retreat and take an opportunity to reflect and feel protected can help them regroup and destress. Similarly, with adult supervision in spaces at school, safety zones at home should also be a space for a parent or guardian to support the child calmly and non-judgmentally, and help them express their feelings, and help guide them toward solutions.

Emotional safety is equally important and includes strategies to establish trust and create a supportive atmosphere.

- Regular "circle time" sessions can encourage expression, connection and developing trust. During these sessions, students sit in a circle and share their thoughts and feelings on various topics. As trust grows within the group, a sense of positive community is built.
- Establishing classroom norms of kindness and respect is an essential strategy to build positive culture and a supportive community. These norms should be developed collaboratively with the students, ensuring that everyone agrees on the importance of kindness, empathy, and respect. Visual reminders, such as posters or charts, can inspire and reinforce these norms, and they serve as constant reminders of the expectations within the classroom.

Community involvement is extremely helpful in creating and maintaining safe spaces.

- Parent volunteer programs provide an excellent way for parents to get involved in the school environment. Parents can assist with supervision in safe zones, help organize trust-building activities, and serve as additional support for children who may be struggling.
- Community workshops covering topics such as cultural sensitivity, empathy training, and strategies for creating inclusive environments can contribute to establishing and reinforcing positive culture.
- By involving the broader community, schools can create a network of support that extends beyond the classroom, ensuring that children feel safe and valued in all areas of their lives, and they are exposed to positivity on a broad level.

The multifaceted approach of creating safe spaces inside and outside of the school environment addresses both physical and emotional safety.

- Establishing designated areas like "quiet rooms" and safe zones in playgrounds, schools can provide immediate havens for children in need.
- Trust-building activities such as regular circle time sessions and the establishment of classroom norms of respect foster an emotionally supportive environment.
- The involvement of the community, through parent volunteer programs and inclusivity workshops, enhances these efforts, creating a comprehensive network of support.

Collectively these strategies can ensure that children feel safe, valued, and respected, both within the school environment, at home, and in the broader community.

5.5 PEER MEDIATION PROGRAMS: STUDENTS HELPING STUDENTS

Peer mediation is a highly effective method designed to help resolve conflicts among students, leveraging the influence of trained peers to mediate disputes.

- Selected students are trained to act as facilitators, helping their peers navigate conflicts and find mutually acceptable solutions.
- These peer mediators are not only skilled in conflict resolution techniques but are also seen as relatable and approachable by their classmates.

- Their role is to guide the disputing parties through a structured process, ensuring that each side is heard and that the outcome is fair and agreed upon by all involved.

Setting up a peer mediation program requires careful planning and execution.

- The first step is selecting suitable students to serve as peer mediators. This selection process should be inclusive, considering students who are respected by their peers and exhibit strong communication skills.
- Once selected, these students undergo comprehensive training.
- Training covers various aspects of conflict resolution, including active listening, empathy, neutrality, and problem-solving.
- Role-playing exercises and workshops can be effective in preparing them for real-life situations.
- After training, clear mediation protocols should be established. These protocols outline the steps to be followed during a mediation session, ensuring consistency and fairness. They typically include guidelines for setting ground rules, facilitating dialogue, and reaching a resolution.

The **benefits of peer mediation** extend beyond resolving individual conflicts.

- Serving as a peer mediator empowers students, helping them develop leadership skills, boosting their confidence and sense of responsibility. These skills are not only valuable in the context of mediation but also contribute to their overall personal growth.

- Peer mediation helps reduce bullying incidents. When students know that their peers are actively involved in resolving conflicts, there is a shift in accountability.
- Peer accountability fosters a more respectful and supportive school environment.
- The presence of peer mediators can deter potential bullies, knowing that their actions are likely to be addressed by their classmates.

Monitoring and evaluating the effectiveness of the peer mediation program is crucial for its sustainability and success.

- **Regular feedback sessions** with peer mediators, teachers, and students involved in mediation can provide valuable insights on identifying strengths and areas for improvement in the program.
- **Tracking conflict resolution outcomes** by maintaining and analyzing records of mediation sessions (i.e. the nature of the conflict, the steps taken during mediation, and the outcomes achieved) can reveal patterns and trends, helping to refine the program further.
- **Regularly reviewing and updating the training and protocols** ensures that the program remains relevant and effective in addressing the evolving needs of the school community.

Peer mediation can significantly improve the school environment by promoting respect, empathy, and accountability. These programs empower students to resolve conflicts, reduce bullying, and build stronger social connections, and the skills gained benefit students well beyond their school years. While implementing and maintaining a peer mediation program requires commitment from the entire school community, the lasting positive impact makes it well worth the effort.

In this chapter, we've explored various practical intervention strategies that parents and teachers can use to address bullying effectively.

- The strategies of immediate responses, open communication, thorough documentation and the creation of safe spaces provide a comprehensive approach for teachers and parents to addressing bullying.
- Peer mediation programs, with their focus on student-led conflict resolution, further enhance these efforts by fostering a supportive and accountable school environment.

As we move forward, we'll explore some real-life case studies and examples, illustrating the application and impact of these strategies in various settings.

YOUR VOICE CAN HELP OTHERS

"The best way to find yourself is to lose yourself in the service of others."

MAHATMA GANDHI

Kindness grows when we share it. When we give our time to help others—even in small ways—the world becomes brighter for everyone.

If you had the opportunity, would you give your time to help another parent, teacher, or student who might be struggling with bullying?

Something we've run into more times than we can count is that the majority of adults, no matter how well-meaning, have no idea how to help a child who's being bullied. Parents hope that it will never happen to their child, and when it does, they're at a loss as to what to do to stop it. Many times, teachers and other well-meaning adults don't have a system in place or protocols to follow, so they don't know where to begin to help.

Our mission with this book is to make understanding—and stopping—bullying clear, practical, and filled with hope. We want to help parents, teachers, and other adults with strategies and tools to help children.

How can YOU help now?

Most people decide which books to read based on comments and reviews. By taking just a moment to share your honest thoughts about "BULLYING–A Comprehensive Guide for Parents, Teachers & Mentors," you could inspire someone in the perfect moment who needs encouragement. Your words could make a life-changing difference for...

- *one more parent who's worried about their child.*
- *one more teacher searching for helpful strategies and tools.*
- *one more student who wants the courage to stand up.*
- *one more family hoping for peace.*
- *one more community ready to spread kindness and create positive change.*

By leaving your comments, you'll make it easier for more parents, teachers, and mentors to find this powerful guide, and you'll encourage them to equip themselves with the tools they need to handle bullying effectively.

Let's support the children in our lives at home and at school, and create the momentum to break the bullying cycle for good...TOGETHER.

We're truly grateful for your voice and your support!

https://www.amazon.com/review/review-your-purchases/?asin=
1962863077

CHAPTER 6
CASE STUDIES & EXAMPLES
SUCCESS STORIES OF INTERVENTION AND SUPPORT AT SCHOOL AND AT HOME

The following collection of case studies highlights both the challenges children face and the meaningful progress that can result from intentional action and consistent support. From overcoming cyberbullying to successful peer intervention, school-wide initiatives, and effective parental involvement, these stories provide practical strategies and proven approaches that inspire hope and empowerment. They show what's possible when the right steps are taken, and serve as a reminder that preventing and addressing bullying requires a proactive, collective effort. Whether you're a parent, teacher, mentor, or school leader, these case studies can offer encouragement, inspiration, and guidance to help you make a lasting, positive impact.

6.1 CASE STUDY: OVERCOMING CYBERBULLYING

Olivia was a typical middle school student, known for her cheerful disposition and active participation in honor society, student government, and cheer leading. She was well-liked by her peers and teachers, excelling both academically and socially. However, her world took a dark turn when she became the target of cyberbullying.

The bullying started with anonymous harassment in response to cheerleading photos she posted on her social media platforms. Fake profiles were posting insulting comments on her current and previous posts, and then malicious rumors, daily threats, and hurtful private messages began flooding her inbox. These relentless attacks began to take a toll on Olivia's mental health and well-being. She became increasingly anxious, fearful of what she might find each time she checked her phone, and she began withdrawing from her friends and favorite activities.

Olivia's first reaction was to keep the bullying to herself, fearing that telling someone might make the situation worse. However, her parents soon noticed the changes in her behavior, she was spending more and more time alone in her room, and they began asking her questions and eventually coaxed the truth from her.

Olivia's mother immediately reported the harassment to the social media platforms involved, hoping that the accounts would be taken down swiftly. Unfortunately, the response from these platforms was slow, and the anonymous nature of the threats made it difficult to track down the perpetrators.

Olivia's school was notified next. The school administrators and counselor took the matter seriously, and took action to meet with Olivia to offer her support. However, they faced significant hurdles in addressing online bullying that occurred outside school hours and off school property.

In response to these challenges, Olivia's parents took a multi-faceted approach to address the cyberbullying.

Digital safety measures were the first line of defense. Olivia's parents helped her block the offending accounts, and they also installed parental control software to monitor her online activity and filter out harmful content.

The school provided counseling and emotional support to help Olivia cope with the psychological impact of the bullying. Regular sessions with the school counselor gave Olivia a safe space to express her fears and anxieties, and she was taught coping strategies to manage her stress.

The intervention strategies began to yield positive results. Olivia gradually regained her confidence and started participating in school activities again. The bullying incidents decreased significantly as the offending accounts were blocked and reported. The counseling sessions helped Olivia develop the emotional strength and resilience to handle any residual harassment with greater ease. The school also took this opportunity to strengthen its policies on cyberbullying. They introduced digital literacy workshops to educate students about the risks of online interactions and the importance of digital citizenship. Teachers received training on recognizing signs of cyberbullying and responding effectively with guidance and support.

The resolution of Olivia's situation offers several key reminders.

- **Prompt and proactive intervention** by parents and schools is crucial in addressing cyberbullying. Olivia's parents' immediate actions to block and report the harassing accounts helped curb the bullying.
- **Providing emotional support** through counseling can significantly aid in the victim's recovery. Olivia's sessions with the school counselor were instrumental in helping her regain her emotional balance.
- **Strengthening school policies and educating students** about digital safety can prevent future incidents. The school's efforts to introduce digital literacy workshops and train teachers created a more informed and vigilant environment, reducing the likelihood of similar cases occurring.

Olivia's story highlights the pervasive nature of cyberbullying and the importance of a comprehensive response. **By combining digital safety practices, emotional support, and ongoing education, both parents and schools can play a key role in addressing and preventing cyberbullying.**

Exercise: Digital Safety Checklist

To support parents and teachers in promoting online safety, this Digital Safety Checklist is based on guidelines from

StopBullying.gov, Common Sense Media, and the Cyberbullying Research Center.

- **Maximize privacy settings** on all social media, gaming, and messaging platforms.
- **Regularly review and update blocked and restricted users** on your child's accounts.
- **Use parental control tools or monitoring software** to stay informed about online activity while respecting your child's growing independence.
- **Educate children about protecting personal information**, including full names, locations, school details, passwords, and photos.
- **Encourage open, judgment-free communication** about online experiences—both positive and negative.
- **Discuss the permanence of online content**, including how posts, photos, and messages can be saved or shared without permission.
- **Teach children how to identify and report cyberbullying**, harassment, or inappropriate content on every platform they use.
- **Establish screen time limits and device-free zones**, especially during meals and before bed, to promote healthy digital habits.
- **Model responsible digital behavior**—children are more likely to follow safe practices when they see adults doing the same.
- **Stay informed about the platforms your child uses**, including emerging apps and games, to better understand potential risks and features.

- **Create a digital safety agreement** as a family or classroom to set clear expectations and promote shared responsibility.

6.2 CASE STUDY: PEER INTERVENTION SUCCESS STORIES

Peer intervention has become a powerful strategy in addressing bullying in schools. When students are empowered to speak up and step in, they not only help stop harmful behavior in the moment but also contribute to building a culture of accountability and respect. Giving students the tools and confidence to intervene makes them active partners in creating a safe, inclusive environment. This sense of responsibility and ownership over their school community reduces the likelihood of bullying before it even starts. By equipping students to take action, we're not just addressing immediate problems—we're nurturing values that promote empathy, leadership, and long-term change.

A specific example of successful peer intervention took place at a high school where a group of students formed a peer support group known as the "Student Allies." The group was made up of students from various grades, all trained in conflict resolution and peer mediation. Their mission was to support their classmates by intervening in bullying incidents and providing a safe space for those affected.

One notable peer intervention involved a bullying incident in their school cafeteria. Alex, a ninth grade band student, was being taunted and harassed by a group of four tenth grade boys. They surrounded him, took his lunch, grabbed his trumpet case and backpack, and threw everything in the trash can. The Student Allies, who had been trained to recognize and address such situations, noticed the interaction from the other side of the cafeteria, and immediately stepped in. They approached the bullies, and asked them to stop, calmly talking to them, while simultaneously a few of the members escorted Alex to a different table, offering him companionship and support, helping him retrieve his belongings.

The success of this peer intervention was not solely due to the actions of the students. Teachers, staff, and administrators had received specialized training on how to support peer intervention initiatives. Training included guidance on how to recognize the signs of bullying, how to facilitate peer mediation sessions, and how to support the Student Allies without undermining their authority. Teachers and staff provided continuous mentorship to the members of the peer support group, helping them navigate a variety of challenging situations and allowing them to refine their intervention skills.

Parents were informed about the peer support group's mission and were encouraged to talk with their children at home about the importance of empathy, speaking up, and supporting others. Their involvement further reinforced the effectiveness of the initiative.

This strong collaboration between teachers, parents, and students created a unified system of support—one that supported their school culture and its core values of respect, accountability, and shared responsibility.

School-wide, the presence of the Student Allies acted as a deterrent to potential bullies, the number of reported bullying incidents dropped, and the student body as a whole became more supportive of the initiative. Students reported feeling safer and more willing to stand up for one another knowing they had the backing of the Student Allies and the school administration. They reported feeling a greater sense of community and belonging, and the overall atmosphere of the school became more positive and inclusive.

The success of the Student Allies program illustrates the powerful impact of peer intervention in addressing bullying and fostering a supportive school environment. **By empowering students to act, providing continuous support from teachers and parents, and building a culture of accountability, schools can significantly reduce bullying incidents and create a safer, more inclusive environment for all students.**

6.3 CASE STUDY: EFFECTIVE SCHOOL-WIDE PROGRAMS

One of the most effective strategies to combat bullying is through a comprehensive, school-wide approach. A standout example is the KiVa program in Finland, developed at the University of Turku. KiVA stands for "against bullying" in Finnish, and the program was developed as a comprehensive approach to create a safe school environment

Its primary goals were to reduce bullying incidents, improve the overall school culture, and support the mental well-being of students. The program incorporates a school curriculum with role-playing exercises to increase empathy among students, computer simulations to encourage proactive intervention as well as integrating strong school policies designed to protect students and foster an inclusive environment.

Implementing the KiVa program required thoughtful planning and strong coordination. The school administration began by conducting comprehensive needs assessments and evaluations to better understand the specific challenges and patterns of bullying within their environment. This groundwork allowed them to design the program to appropriately meet the needs of their student population.

Following the initial assessment, the next step was extensive training for teachers and staff. The training covered the core principles of the program, how to identify and respond to bullying, and effective action strategies for supporting both victims and aggressors. Educators were equipped with practical tools and guidance to integrate the curriculum into their daily lessons.

To introduce the program to students, the school organized interactive and engaging workshops and assemblies. These sessions featured hands-on activities and meaningful discussions designed to promote empathy, respect, and encourage students to take a stand against bullying.

Despite its structured, thoughtful planned approach, the implementation of the program did face challenges. Resistance from some staff members created hurdles. Some were skeptical of the program's effectiveness, while others were resistant to shifting away from familiar routines. In response, the school provided additional information, resources and training around their concerns, as well as ongoing education and support to help them feel more confident and comfortable with the new methods.

Student engagement was another area of focus. While many students embraced the program enthusiastically, others were indifferent or resistant. To boost student participation, the school began incorporating student suggestions and feedback into the program design and made sessions more interactive and relatable to their everyday experiences. Parental involvement was encouraged with informational meetings and workshops to educate families and build broader support for the initiative.

Within a year of implementing the KiVa program, the school reported a significant decline in bullying incidents. **Consistent messaging throughout the school and home communities as well as a supportive school culture helped create an environment where students felt safer and more connected.** Students expressed greater confidence in standing up to bullying, while parents reported improvements in their children's emotional well-being and social interactions. Overall, the school climate improved significantly, and the program was considered a success.

6.4 CASE STUDY: PARENTAL INVOLVEMENT IN BULLYING PREVENTION

One of the most powerful ways parents can help in bullying prevention is by fostering open, judgment-free communication. Creating a safe space where children feel comfortable sharing their experiences (e.g. regular check-ins, asking about their day, and genuinely listening) helps build a strong foundation of trust. When children feel heard and supported without judgment, they are much more likely to speak up about bullying and seek help when they need it.

Equally important is maintaining a strong partnership with the school. When parents actively engage with teachers and administrators, they can more effectively advocate for their child's safety and emotional well-being. This collaboration between home and school creates a consistent, united front against bullying and sends a powerful message to the child: they are supported, and they don't have to face challenges alone.

Consider the case of Jessica, a mother who took thoughtful and proactive steps when her son, Ethan, became the target of harassment and bullying. Ethan, a bright and sensitive fifth grader, began coming home with a noticeable change in his demeanor. He grew unusually quiet, retreated to his room by himself, he was apprehensive about going to school, and often appeared anxious. Jessica gently but consistently asked him questions about school and how he was feeling, and after several conversations, Ethan opened up to her about how everyday the boys who sat behind him in math class relentlessly poked him with pencils leaving holes in his shirts and sometimes wounds in his skin. They called him shorty, and mocked his lisp. They told other kids to leave him out of games at recess and invited everyone in his class except him to their birthday parties. Recognizing the seriousness of the situation, Jessica decided to take action, not only to support her son, but to spark change in the community.

She organized a community-wide anti-bullying event, bringing parents, teachers, and local experts together to attend discussions, raise awareness, share strategies, and inspire a unified commitment to addressing the bullying issue.

At the same time, she scheduled meetings with the school administrators and teachers, shared documented incidents, and clearly expressed her concerns not only for her child but for other students who were struggling. Her efforts prompted the school to reevaluate its anti-bullying policies and initiate staff training focused on recognizing and responding to bullying more effectively.

In addition, she volunteered to organize special events and help implement new student programs designed to build a more inclusive school culture. She spoke to teachers about offering new clubs that could encourage inclusion of a wide range of kids, and one teacher even offered to develop a peer mentoring program to help other students with challenges. Jessica's collaboration with the school illustrated the powerful role that parents can play in creating positive change within educational systems.

At home, Jessica implemented several helpful strategies to support Ethan. Encouraging him to journal, daily check-ins and conversations gave Ethan a safe space to share his thoughts and feelings. Through consistent empathetic listening and reassurance, she helped Ethan feel seen, heard, and supported. To rebuild his confidence, she encouraged him to gradually re-engage in activities he loved, helping to strengthen his social connections and sense of self.

Beyond emotional support, Jessica advocated for stronger school policies, pushing for clear reporting procedures and consistent consequences for bullying. Her advocacy led to the formation of the student support team which included counselors and peer mentors dedicated to helping students who experience bullying.

Jessica's dedicated efforts led to the school environment becoming more supportive, and bullying incidents declined. The anti-bullying workshop sparked ongoing dialogue and positive communication among parents and educators, encouraging a more proactive and unified response to bullying. Students began to realize that the adults around them were committed to their well-being. For Ethan, the changes were life-changing. With his mother's unwavering support and the safety he now felt in school, he regained his confidence, became more socially engaged, and began to heal from the emotional impact of bullying.

Jessica's story illustrates the important role parents can play in bullying prevention and intervention. **Through open communi-**

cation, active collaboration with schools, and consistent advocacy, parents can make a lasting difference, not just for their own children, but for the entire school community.

6.5 CASE STUDY: MENTAL HEALTH SUPPORT LEADING TO RESOLUTION

Bullying can leave deep emotional wounds, often resulting in anxiety, depression, and other lasting psychological effects. Addressing these emotional impacts is a critical part of helping students recover and regain their sense of well-being.

Professional counseling offers a safe, structured environment where children can express their feelings, process their experiences, and learn healthy coping strategies. This kind of support helps in rebuilding self-esteem, restoring confidence, and fostering long-term resilience.

Consider the case of Jake, a high school sophomore who experienced severe anxiety and depression after being subjected to persistent verbal and physical attacks . Jake, an honor society student and a talented artist, had once been confident and engaged. He would attend weekend gatherings, sporting events and participate in after school art and game clubs almost every day. However, an incident at a party with a group of girls changed everything. A heated discussion about something very minor led to personal insults and others getting involved in the argument. Soon, rumors and lies began spreading about what was said, and Jake became the scapegoat, being blamed and accused of insults he never said. This then evolved to a campaign of relentless verbal and physical harassment from friends of friends, and some people he didn't even know. Over time, Jake's sense of safety eroded. His academic performance declined, and he began to withdraw socially, avoiding both school and activities he once enjoyed. Alarmed by the changes in their son, Jake's parents reached out to the school, which led to a referral to the school counselor.

Jake's journey toward healing involved a comprehensive plan to help and support him. The school counselor began meeting with him regularly, providing a space where he could talk openly and begin working through his feelings about the struggles. Sessions focused on expressing his thoughts and feelings and developing practical coping skills, deep breathing exercises, mindfulness techniques, and thought reframing. These tools helped Jake manage his anxiety and helped him shift his perspective.

In addition to individual counseling, the school offered a peer support program for students affected by bullying. Peer support groups gave Jake a much-needed sense of belonging and understanding from fellow students. Hearing others share their stories of similar struggles helped him feel less alone and more hopeful.

With time and consistent mental health support, Jake began to rediscover his light, his voice, regain his confidence, and re-engage with school life. His story is a powerful reminder that addressing the emotional impact of bullying is just as important as stopping the behavior itself. **When mental health is prioritized alongside prevention efforts at school and at home, they create a healing environment where students can heal and recover.**

CHAPTER 7
PARENT, TEACHER & COMMUNITY COLLABORATION

HELPING CHILDREN PROCESS EMOTIONS & REBUILD CONFIDENCE THROUGH LOVE, REASSURANCE & POSITIVE ACTION

Creating a school culture where bullying is taken seriously, with active prevention protocols, immediate responses and ongoing follow-up requires more than good intentions. It requires establishing clear policies, training staff effectively, encouraging open communication between school and home, and fostering strong partnerships with supportive resources in the community. This chapter provides a practical framework for schools and families to collaborate effectively in pursuit of this shared mission.

7.1 CREATING ANTI-BULLYING POLICIES: GUIDELINES

Clearly defined anti-bullying policies lay the foundation for a safe, positive, and respectful school culture. When guidelines are well understood, widely communicated, and consistently enforced, everyone—students, staff, and families—is empowered to respond quickly and take appropriate action when necessary. The following strategies highlight key components of policies that are effective, practical, and easy to implement.

- **Establish a clear, shared definition of bullying.** A well-defined and consistently used explanation helps everyone in the school community—students, staff, and families—understand what bullying is and recognize it in its different forms. For example, *physical bullying* includes hitting or pushing, *verbal bullying* involves name-calling or teasing, *relational bullying* can mean spreading rumors or excluding someone on purpose, and *cyberbullying* may take the form of hurtful messages or social media harassment. This clarity ensures that inappropriate behaviors are not overlooked or mislabeled and prompt appropriate action can be taken.
- **Include specific behavioral expectations.** Clearly outlining acceptable and unacceptable behaviors helps create consistency and accountability across the school community. For example, *expected/acceptable behaviors* listed may include using respectful language, including others in group activities, and reporting harmful behavior

to a trusted adult. *Unacceptable behaviors* might include physical or emotional harassment, name-calling, spreading rumors, deliberately excluding peers, or posting hurtful messages online. By listing and defining behaviors in specific, concrete terms, it will help to ensure everyone understands the standards and consequences.

- **Outline clear reporting procedures.** Provide straightforward protocols and step-by-step instructions for students, parents, and staff on how to report bullying incidents. This should include who to contact (e.g., counselor, principal, or designated staff member), what information to provide, sample documentation forms, and what to expect after a report is made. Be sure to also include options for anonymous reporting, such as a secure dropbox, online form, or hotline, to ensure that students who fear retaliation still have a safe way to speak up. A great time for this information to be discussed with teachers and staff would be professional training days before the school year begins and announced to parents through end of summer emails and discussions at back to school events.
- **Define consequences and interventions.** Establish a tiered system of consequences and interventions based on the severity, intent, and frequency of the behavior. For example, a first-time verbal offense might warrant an immediate discussion with the student and notification of the parent, while repeated or severe bullying could lead to counseling, disciplinary action, or suspension. These procedures should be clearly outlined, thoroughly discussed with administrators, and clearly communicated to staff, parents, and students. Refer to county or state guidelines, as there may already be recommended

procedures in place. Clearly defining the steps and protocols will help ensure consistency, fairness, and transparency in how bullying is addressed.

- **Ensure accessibility and visibility.** Make sure the anti-bullying policy is easy to find and understand. It should be included in student handbooks, posted clearly in classrooms, hallways, and common areas, and available online in multiple languages if needed. Schools can also review the policy with students, staff and parents several times throughout the school year during classtime, assemblies, staff meetings, or parent email campaigns to keep expectations fresh in everyone's minds.
- **Engage students, parents, and educators.** Involve everyone who has a stake in the bullying issue in the development, review, and implementation of bullying prevention policies. This can include student/parent/teacher surveys, parent-teacher meetings, student focus groups, or school-wide forums. When those directly affected by school policies have a voice in shaping them, they are more likely to support and uphold those policies, creating a stronger sense of ownership and accountability.

7.2 TRAINING SCHOOL STAFF: RECOGNIZING AND ADDRESSING BULLYING

Even the best-written policy and procedures is ineffective if the staff is not well-trained and prepared. Regular training and informational refreshers and reminders will keep educators equipped with the tools and confidence to recognize bullying and respond promptly and appropriately. The following strategies are recommended for ongoing professional development and collaborative learning.

- **Provide annual training.** Regular training will keep staff informed on current best practices for identifying and handling bullying behavior.
    - *Examples: Host yearly workshops where staff learn updated bullying prevention recommendations, protocols, and review recent trends such as cyberbullying tactics. Host parent workshops as well, to keep them informed of current recommendations. Keeping parents connected will unify efforts at home and school to maximize the effectiveness of all strategies.*
- **Teach intervention strategies.** Empower staff with protocols and practical tools to de-escalate situations and support students effectively.
    - *Examples: During training meetings, teachers are taught specific de-escalation phrases such as "Let's pause and take a breath" or "I hear both of you; let's step aside to talk" to help calmly separate students in conflict. They also learn body language cues, such as standing with open posture, maintaining a neutral facial expression, and positioning themselves slightly between the students without appearing confrontational. In addition, role-playing exercises allow staff to practice approaching students slowly, lowering their voice, and using gentle hand gestures to signal safety and control. These strategies give teachers the tools to diffuse tension quickly while keeping students safe and avoiding escalation.*
- **Use real-life scenarios and role-playing.** Being aware of various scenarios and practicing responses through role-

playing helps staff build confidence and develop the skills they need to take effective action in real-life situations.

- *Examples: Allow opportunities in training sessions where staff role-play responding to both verbal and physical bullying scenarios. For verbal bullying, teachers can practice calmly approaching the students, using de-escalation phrases like "I can see there's a disagreement; let's talk about this separately" and then modeling restorative follow-up conversations with each student. For physical bullying scenarios, staff can practice positioning themselves safely between students, giving firm, clear directives such as "Stop—move apart now" while signaling for additional support if needed..*

- **Train staff on documentation protocols.** Training and emphasis on proper documentation protocols promotes accurate and timely reporting of incidents to ensure effective school responses.
  - *Examples: Staff are provided with samples of properly completed incident reports and trained on the importance of submitting them immediately after a bullying event. Prompt reporting ensures consistent and accurate record-keeping and allows schools to take timely follow-up actions, such as notifying parents and connecting students with additional support like counseling or peer mediation resources.*

- **Foster a shared responsibility culture.** Create a culture where everyone—administrators, teachers, staff, and families—actively contributes to bullying prevention by staying informed, understanding the issues and procedures, and taking consistent, responsible action when necessary.
  - *Example: The school launches a "One Team Against Bullying" initiative where teachers, parents, staff, and*

community members commit to clear, coordinated steps to prevent and address bullying. In this intiative, the school announces simple reporting tools such as an easily accessible online form, dedicated email address, and anonymous drop box locations, so everyone knows how and where to report concerns. Staff receive regular training on prevention strategies, early warning signs and response protocols. Parents receive resource guides electronically or in print to support children at home. A system is also put in place to track reports and follow up quickly, ensuring no incident is overlooked.

7.3 IMPLEMENTING RESTORATIVE PRACTICES: REPAIRING HARM AND RESTORING RELATIONSHIPS

Restorative practices shift the focus from discipline and punishment to growth, reflection, and connection. These approaches help strengthen relationships and foster a more compassionate school climate. By guiding students to reflect on their behavior, understand the impact of their actions, take responsibility, and make amends, restorative practices promote healing and rebuild trust. The following strategies offer practical ways to implement restorative methods within school environments.

- **Facilitate "restorative circles" or conferences.** Create structured, facilitated group discussions where those involved in a conflict or incident can share their perspectives, listen to one another, reflect on the impact, and work together toward resolution and healing, with defined accountable action steps.

- **Focus on accountability and empathy.** Teach students to take responsibility for their actions by recognizing how their behavior affects others, fostering a deeper sense of compassion and emotional awareness. This can be taught in small group/classroom discussions as well as school-wide assemblies throughout the year. Encouraging these discussions at home will also help to reinforce principles and keep parents and teachers unified in their efforts with consistent messaging.
- **Encourage student-led resolutions.** Involve students in developing solutions and agreements after a conflict, helping them take ownership of their behavior and promoting maturity, self-reflection, and accountability.
- **Train facilitators.** Provide training to staff or involve designated leaders with specialized training in restorative techniques to ensure the process is handled appropriately — with respect, neutrality, and beneficial to all participants.
- **Monitor outcomes.** Follow-up and track progress, making adjustments if necessary. The goal is to ensure that the resolution is successful, relationships are improving, and behavior changes are sustained over time.

7.4 MONITORING AND EVALUATION: ENSURING POLICY EFFECTIVENESS

Ongoing assessment is crucial for ensuring that anti-bullying efforts are working. By analyzing data and listening to feedback, schools can fine-tune their strategies and respond to new challenges. The following strategies can be effective tools for evaluating progress and making continuous improvements.

- **Conduct regular culture/climate surveys.** Gather honest feedback from students and staff about bullying, safety, and overall school culture to identify concerns early and guide necessary improvement efforts.
- **Analyze incident reports.** Review documented cases to identify trends, high-risk areas, or recurring issues, allowing for targeted and timely interventions.
- **Review and update policies annually.** Ensure that anti-bullying policies stay relevant, effective, and aligned with evolving student needs and legal requirements.
- **Set measurable goals.** Establish clear objectives, such as reducing bullying incidents or increasing students' sense of safety, to track progress and maintain accountability.
- **Use feedback loops.** Regularly incorporate input from students, staff, and families into decisions, strengthening trust, transparency, and the relevance of school strategies.

7.5 PARENT-TEACHER COLLABORATION: BUILDING TRUST AND OPEN COMMUNICATION

Parents and teachers are essential partners in bullying prevention. Open communication builds trust, ensures early intervention, and fosters a consistent message of care and accountability. This section explores how schools can engage families and promote mutual understanding.

- **Create regular communication channels.** Use newsletters, school apps, online portals, and scheduled meetings to keep parents consistently informed and engaged in school activities and updates.

- **Encourage two-way communication.** Provide opportunities for parents to share their perspectives, ask questions, and collaborate with teachers, creating a stronger partnership.
- **Hold parent education workshops.** Offer informative sessions that teach families about bullying prevention, digital safety, and how to support their child's emotional development.
- **Provide clear guidance.** Outline specific steps for reporting bullying and offer tips on how parents can support their children emotionally and practically.
- **Reinforce shared values.** Align messages from home and school by consistently promoting respect, kindness, and accountability, helping children internalize these values.

7.6 COORDINATED STRATEGIES: ALIGNING EFFORTS BETWEEN HOME AND SCHOOL

Consistency between home and school reinforces expectations and supports student growth. When families and educators align their approaches, children feel supported, safe, and are more likely to adopt positive behaviors. The following strategies offer practical ways to coordinate interventions and share tools.

- **Develop shared language and expectations.** Using consistent terminology and behavior standards at school and at home reinforces important concepts and helps students better understand expectations and respond more confidently across environments.
  - *Example: School, teachers and family all use the phrases "take a respectful pause" or "let's take a few deep breaths" to help a student manage frustration. This consistency will*

help reinforce effective and positive calming strategies in both places.

- **Collaborate on student behavior plans.** When parents and educators work together to create and implement behavior plans, students receive consistent support and guidance in both settings, reinforcing positive change.
  - *Example: Through effective communication between school and home, a student who struggles with following directions, settling, or focusing can benefit from using the same visual cue system—such as hand signals—both in class and at home, helping them stay more focused and on task.*
- **Include parents in restorative practices.** Inviting families to participate in restorative conversations fosters a collaborative and unified approach to resolving conflict, promoting healing and shared accountability.
  - *Example: After a playground incident, a restorative circle includes the student, their parent, and school staff, allowing everyone to discuss, reflect, talk about resolutions, and move forward together.*
- **Share tools and resources.** Providing families with social-emotional learning resources and tools allows them to practice and reinforce important skills at home, extending the benefits of proven school-based programs into everyday life outside of school.
  - *Example: Teachers send home summary sheets such as a "feelings chart" or journaling exercises used in class so families can use it during evening routines and conversations to reinforce and support emotional awareness introduced at school.*
- **Celebrate joint successes.** Acknowledging progress and achievements together builds a sense of unity between

home and school, reinforcing positive behaviors and creating a more connected, supportive community.

- ○ *Example: A student's improvement in conflict resolution is recognized in class or at a school assembly, as well as a family celebration dinner, reinforcing the consistency of pride felt by the educators and parents supporting the child.*

7.7 COMMUNITY INVOLVEMENT: ENGAGING LOCAL RESOURCES AND ADVOCACY

Preventing bullying is a shared responsibility that extends beyond the school walls. Partnering with community organizations brings in valuable expertise, advocacy, and resources. The following strategies can help schools build alliances to strengthen prevention efforts and foster a culture of respect.

- **Partner with local organizations.** Collaborating with mental health agencies, youth services, or advocacy groups expands access to expert resources and reinforces a shared commitment to student safety and well-being.
- **Invite guest speakers.** Bringing in professionals such as counselors, motivational speakers, or individuals with personal bullying experiences introduces new perspectives and strengthens awareness and empathy among students and staff.
- **Create community coalitions.** Forming partnerships between schools, families, law enforcement, and community leaders builds a united front against bullying and enhances communication and accountability.
- **Host school-wide events.** Organizing assemblies, awareness campaigns, or kindness challenges engages the

broader school community and promotes a culture of inclusion, respect, and collective responsibility.

- **Advocate for policy change.** Supporting or initiating improvements to district or state-level bullying policies ensures broader systemic change, helping to protect more students and reinforce consistent standards across schools.

CHAPTER 8
DIGITAL SAFETY & CYBERBULLYING

HOW TO HELP YOUR CHILDREN WHEN THEY ARE BULLIED—EVEN WHEN IT OCCURS ONLINE

In today's digital age, harassment and bullying no longer ends at the schoolyard. With widespread access to social media, messaging apps, and online gaming, children are increasingly exposed to cyberbullying—harassment that can occur 24/7 and follow them into their homes. As a result, parents, educators, and caregivers must understand the risks and take proactive steps to protect children online.

This chapter outlines practical guidance for parents, teachers, and schools on how to protect children online, foster responsible digital behavior, and respond effectively to incidents of cyberbullying.

8.1 UNDERSTANDING CYBERBULLYING: ONLINE HARASSMENT AND ITS IMPACT

Cyberbullying refers to the use of digital technologies—such as social media, messaging apps, or gaming platforms—to harass, threaten, or embarrass others. Understanding the scope and impact of online harassment is the first step in preventing and addressing it.

- **Recognize the different forms of cyberbullying.** Cyberbullying can appear in many forms, including sending mean texts, spreading online rumors, impersonating someone, excluding individuals from digital groups, or sharing private information without consent.
- **Acknowledge the emotional and psychological toll.** Children and teens affected by cyberbullying may suffer from increased anxiety, depression, withdrawal from social settings, and lower self-esteem, which can impact their academic and emotional development.
- **Understand the permanence and reach of digital harm.** Online content can spread quickly and remain accessible indefinitely, increasing the long-term impact of bullying.
- **Know the warning signs.** Be alert for changes in behavior such as mood swings, avoidance of technology, a sudden drop in grades, or loss of interest in activities, which may signal distress.

- **Promote empathy and awareness.** Teaching students about the real impact of their online behavior helps foster empathy and can reduce the likelihood of engaging in or tolerating harmful behavior.

8.2 DIGITAL SAFETY MEASURES: PROTECTING CHILDREN ONLINE

Establishing strong safety protocols helps minimize children's exposure to online risks. Proactive digital safety measures provide the foundation for safe and healthy technology use. The following are effective strategies to help prevent online issues.

- **Use parental controls and privacy settings.** Setting and maintaining strict parental controls and privacy settings helps restrict access to inappropriate content, manage screen time, and protect personal data on devices and apps from strangers and other entities.
- **Teach password safety and privacy awareness.** Teach and reinforce the importance of creating strong, unique passwords, never sharing login details, and regularly updating privacy settings on all platforms. Note: Adults (i.e. parents, teachers, etc.) should be in charge of setting passwords and privacy settings on all devices.
- **Encourage open communication about online activity.** Foster honest conversations with children about their digital experiences to build trust and provide guidance through any challenges they encounter online. Let them know they can talk to you without fear of punishment or judgment, which increases the likelihood they'll speak up if something upsetting happens.

- **Limit unsupervised device use.** Establish clear screen time boundaries and encourage device use only in shared family or public educational spaces to support healthy habits and ongoing supervision.
- **Review apps, games, and digital footprints together.** Make it a routine to check privacy policies, review friend lists, and discuss app content to ensure children are engaging with safe, age-appropriate digital environments. If children learn that this is an expected and enforced rule with consequences if broken, it will become an established and respected boundary.
- **Model safe and respectful tech behavior.** Your actions set a powerful example. When adults pause before posting, prioritize face-to-face interaction, and maintain healthy screen habits, children are more likely to mirror those behaviors. Demonstrate responsible use of technology, showing children how to engage online with awareness, respect, and balance.

8.3 ONLINE BEHAVIORS: MONITORING AND MANAGING FOR SAFETY

Monitoring online behavior doesn't mean constant surveillance—it means staying involved, creating healthy boundaries, and teaching kids to navigate the digital world responsibly. The following strategies can help parents and educators manage online behavior in ways that foster both safety and trust.

- **Regularly check devices and apps.** Stay updated on which platforms your child uses, the types of content they access, and who they're communicating with to ensure their online environment is safe.

- **Review browser history and friend lists.** Periodic checks of browsing history and online contacts can help identify potential exposure to harmful content or interactions that require adult guidance.
- **Discuss consequences of online actions.** Help children understand that their digital behavior—what they post, share, or say—can have lasting effects on their reputation, relationships, and emotional well-being.
- **Teach how to report and block.** Equip children with practical skills to protect themselves, such as how to block users who behave inappropriately and how to report harmful content to trusted adults and platform moderators.
- **Balance oversight with trust.** Maintain a supportive and respectful approach by setting clear digital boundaries while allowing age-appropriate independence, reinforcing your role as a guide rather than a watchdog.

8.4 TEACHING DIGITAL CITIZENSHIP: BUILDING RESPONSIBILITY AND RESPECT ONLINE

Digital citizenship is more than knowing how to use technology—it's about using it with integrity, responsibility, and awareness. As children engage more deeply in digital spaces, it's essential they understand how their words and actions online impact others and shape their own reputations.

By integrating digital citizenship education at home and in the classroom, adults can help students develop the skills they need to navigate the digital world safely and responsibly. The following strategies can help to encourage responsible online behaviors and develop digital citizenship.

- **Promote respectful communication.** Teach children to interact online with the same kindness and empathy expected in face-to-face conversations, emphasizing that words typed behind a screen can hurt just as much as those spoken aloud and can have an even longer lasting effect.
- **Highlight digital footprints.** Help students understand that everything they post online—photos, comments, or messages—can have a lasting impact and may be seen by future schools, employers, or peers.
- **Discuss online reputation.** Encourage children to think carefully before posting, reminding them that even seemingly harmless content can be misinterpreted or shared beyond their intended audience. Everything has the potential to be shared, screen shot and become permanently online, even if it has been deleted.
- **Incorporate into classroom lessons.** Weave digital citizenship into everyday learning by using practical examples, discussions, and hands-on activities that help students connect responsible online behavior with their real-life experiences.
- **Celebrate positive digital behavior.** Recognize and reward students who demonstrate kindness, responsibility, and respect online, reinforcing the idea that good digital behavior matters and makes a difference.

8.5 RESPONDING TO CYBERBULLYING: GUIDANCE FOR PARENTS AND EDUCATORS

When cyberbullying occurs, the way adults respond can make a significant difference in how a child responds and recovers. Whether you're a parent, teacher, or caregiver, it's important to act with care, urgency, and consistency. These key steps help ensure the child feels supported, the situation is addressed properly, and long-term emotional well-being is prioritized. The following are a few helpful strategies to help guide parents and educators in their responses.

- **Remain calm and supportive.** Reassure the child that they are not alone, the bullying is not their fault, and you are there to help them through it.
- **Document everything.** Keep accurate, thorough and detailed records. Save screenshots, messages, usernames, and any relevant URLs to use as evidence when reporting the incident to schools or platforms.
- **Report through proper channels.** Notify school administrators, social media platforms, or law enforcement when needed to ensure immediate and appropriate action is taken.
- **Provide emotional support.** Consider counseling or mental health services to help the child process the experience, manage emotions, and rebuild confidence.
- **Follow up consistently.** Continue checking in with the child and coordinating with school staff to make sure the bullying has stopped and long-term, lasting support is in place.

CHAPTER 9
MENTAL HEALTH, INCLUSION & LONG-TERM SUPPORT
HELPING CHILDREN OVERCOME BULLYING RELATED PAIN, LOW SELF-ESTEEM AND SELF-DOUBT

A comprehensive approach to bullying prevention and recovery must include attention to mental health, emotional resilience, inclusivity, and sustained support. This chapter summarizes the emotional and psychological effects of bullying, recommendations to help children recover and grow, and strategies to create inclusive, long-term support systems that can promote lasting change.

9.1 THE EMOTIONAL TOLL OF BULLYING: RECOGNIZING SIGNS AND PROVIDING SUPPORT

Because bullying can leave deep emotional scars affecting a child's self-esteem, behavior, and overall mental health, recognizing the signs early and providing timely support can help prevent long-term psychological consequences.

- **Watch for changes in behavior.** Behaviors such as a sudden drop in academic performance, withdrawal from favorite activities, increased irritability, or reluctance to go to school may indicate that a child is experiencing emotional distress related to bullying. These behavioral shifts are often the first outward signs that something is wrong.
- **Notice physical symptoms.** Unexplained physical complaints such as headaches, stomach aches, or frequent visits to the school nurse can be manifestations of internal stress or anxiety caused by bullying. These symptoms should not be dismissed, as they may reflect deeper emotional issues.
- **Listen carefully to language.** Pay attention to what children say about themselves and others. Comments that suggest self-doubt, fear, worthlessness, or hopelessness can signal emotional harm and should be addressed promptly and compassionately.

- **Create safe spaces for expression.** Providing outlets like journaling, drawing, music, or open, judgment-free conversations allows children to express feelings they may struggle to verbalize. These safe spaces support emotional processing and can help adults better understand what the child is experiencing.

9.2 COUNSELING AND MENTAL HEALTH SERVICES: WHEN AND HOW TO SEEK HELP

Access to professional mental health support can make a critical difference in how a child recovers from bullying or adjusts to school life. Knowing when and how to connect children with help is essential.

- **Refer when signs persist.** If a child continues to show signs of emotional distress such as anxiety, sadness, irritability, or withdrawal for more than a few weeks, connecting them with a licensed counselor or therapist for early intervention can help prevent long-term effects and support healthier coping.
- **Utilize school-based services.** Most schools have access to counselors, psychologists, or social workers who are trained to support students facing emotional or behavioral challenges. These professionals can provide assessments, one-on-one sessions, and referrals to outside services as needed.
- **Involve families in care.** When families are actively engaged in the counseling process, children are more likely to feel supported and make meaningful progress. Collaboration between home and counselor/therapist

helps reinforce coping strategies and maintain consistency in care.

- **Destigmatize mental health support.** When framed as a tool for discovering solutions, building strength, and developing resilience, counseling can empower students to seek help with confidence and without shame. Helping children and families view counseling as a positive, commonly used resource encourages openness and reduces stigma.

9.3 BUILDING EMOTIONAL RESILIENCE: TOOLS AND TECHNIQUES

Resilience is the ability to adapt and recover from adversity, stress, or setbacks. For children who have experienced bullying or other social-emotional challenges, building resilience can be difficult, but it is crucial for their healing and long-term well-being. By providing them with practical tools and nurturing relationships, we can help them develop the confidence, strength, and emotional control needed to navigate life's challenges. The following strategies offer effective ways to support children in building emotional resilience.

- **Teach self-regulation strategies.** These techniques are incredibly powerful, and they can help children in every step of their growth, not just in recovery situations. Introducing techniques such as deep breathing, mindfulness, and grounding exercises can help children calm themselves when feeling nervous, anxious, or overwhelmed. These practices promote emotional control and reduce impulsive reactions. Once they feel calm, other effective exercises can also be implemented, such as techniques to build courage and goal-setting visualizations to help develop confidence.

- ○ *Example 1–**Breathing Exercise**: When students feel frustrated or nervous, teach them a breathing exercise that can help calm them.*
  - ▪ *Breathe in slowly through your nose for a count of 4... hold it for a count of 4...then exhale through your mouth for a count of 4. With each exhale, feel every part of your body relax little by little, starting from the top of your head, all the way down to the tips of your fingers and toes. Do this several times until you feel calmer and more relaxed.*
- ○ *Example 2–**20 Seconds of Courage**: The previous breathing exercise can be used if you are trying to build up the courage to do something challenging, big or small. It could be jumping off the diving board at the pool, talking to new people, or even raising your hand in class.*
  - ▪ *After you have taken your deep breaths, next: give yourself 20 SECONDS to BE BRAVE. Just 20 seconds... to confidently raise your hand in class and ask a question...20 seconds to say "hello" and shake hands with your parent's friend you've never met...or 20 seconds to take that first jump off of the diving board. Once you allow yourself that 20 seconds of bravery, you will be so happy and proud of yourself. Each time you do this, it will help you develop confidence, little by little, and that confidence will be part of you forever.*
- • *Example 3–**Visualization Exercise**: Once you're calm and relaxed after your breathing exercise, you can practice a visualization exercise that will help with achieving goals or completing a challenging task.*

○ *Close your eyes, breathe deeply and slowly. Next, create a crystal clear picture in your mind of yourself already accomplishing your goal. Imagine it to the detail. What does it look like? What sounds do you hear? What do you smell? How happy do you feel? Allow yourself to see it clearly, hear the sounds around you, smell the air, and feel every detail of accomplishing it. Now, ENJOY IT. Truly FEEL the happiness and excitement of your achievement. Once you're able to experience all of that, you begin to BELIEVE you can accomplish it. And when you truly BELIEVE you can do it...that is the moment when CONFIDENCE is born. Confidence will fuel your positive thoughts, behaviors, and actions, which will lead you to important opportunities, achievements, and successes!*

- **Practice problem-solving skills.** Guide children in identifying challenges, brainstorming possible solutions, weighing pros and cons, and making thoughtful decisions. These strategies help build confidence in their ability to handle conflicts and setbacks.
  - ○ *Example: A teacher helps two students resolve a disagreement by walking them through a simple four-step problem-solving worksheet together:*
    - → *Identify the problem – Understand what the disagreement is about.*
    - → *Brainstorm solutions – Come up with possible ways to solve it.*
    - → *Weigh pros & cons – Discuss the benefits/downsides of each solution.*
    - → *Choose the best option – Agree on the most fair and positive approach.*
- **Foster positive self-talk.** Help children become aware of their inner dialogue and intentionally replace negative,

self-critical thoughts with positive, affirming messages. Teaching them to reframe challenges and shift their mindset not only promotes emotional stability but also strengthens their overall self-image and confidence.

  ○ *Example: When a child says, "I'm terrible at math," they're encouraged to reframe it as, "I'm still learning, and I can improve with practice."*

- **Encourage supportive peer relationships.** Encourage children to build and maintain healthy friendships that provide emotional support, encouragement, and a sense of belonging. Positive peer connections can act as a protective buffer against the effects of bullying and isolation.

  ○ *Example: A student struggling with loneliness is paired with a peer buddy during recess, helping them feel more included and connected.*

9.4 SUPPORTING THE BULLIED CHILD AND REDIRECTING THE BULLY

Addressing bullying requires support for both the child who was targeted and the child who exhibited the bullying behavior. Each student has different emotional and behavioral needs, and both deserve guidance to heal, grow, and evolve, so they can each contribute positively to their community in and out of school.

The following strategies promote healing, accountability, and long-term growth for everyone involved:

- **Validate the experience of the bullied child.** Assure them they are heard, believed, and supported without judgment, which helps rebuild trust and emotional safety.

Taking their concerns seriously also encourages future openness and shows that adults are reliable allies in difficult situations. Letting them know they are not alone, and that what happened to them matters can be the first step in their healing process.

- **Create a plan of support.** Collaborate with the child, their family, and school staff to develop a plan aimed at restoring confidence, repairing peer relationships, and monitoring their well-being. This plan may include regular check-ins and conversations with the child to find out how they are feeling, counseling referrals, and opportunities to rebuild social connections through guided peer support meetings and social gatherings. Clearly outlining who will do what, and creating a timeline ensures that the child receives consistent and timely support at home and at school.

- **Redirect harmful behavior.** Help the child who bullied understand the impact of their actions by giving them opportunities to learn and practice empathy, accountability and making amends. Guided reflection exercise, discussions, and role-playing can have a positive impact for change. Strongly encouraging accountability and emotional awareness through counseling and reinforced exercises practiced at home can help prevent repeated behavior and promote healthier ways to relate to others. Offering structured opportunities to learn and demonstrate empathy will help the child replace harmful behavior with constructive, respectful choices.

- **Implement accountability and growth opportunities.** Use restorative practices, counseling, or mentoring to teach new social and emotional skills while holding the student accountable in a constructive and supportive way.

- **Restorative practices.** Strategies such as facilitated conversations, restorative circles, or written reflection letters allow the student to understand the impact of their actions, take responsibility, and make amends in a respectful setting. For example, a guided restorative circle might include the student who caused harm, the student affected, and a trained facilitator, with each participant sharing their feelings and working toward a resolution. Counseling sessions can help the student explore underlying emotions or behavioral patterns, while mentoring programs connect them with trusted adults who can model empathy, self-regulation, and respectful communication. These interventions not only address the immediate behavior but also promote long-term character development, emotional growth, and healthier peer relationships.

9.5 INCLUSIVE PRACTICES FOR DIVERSE STUDENT NEEDS

A positive and inclusive school culture supports students from all backgrounds and perspectives, including those with disabilities, from marginalized communities, or with unique learning or emotional needs.

When students feel accepted, valued, and included, they are more likely to thrive socially, emotionally, and academically.

Inclusion is essential for both bullying prevention and student success, as it fosters compassion, acceptance, and empathy, which reduces isolation and promotes respect for differences.

The following inclusive practices help create a positive culture and respectful, supportive environment where all students feel valued.

- **Acknowledge and celebrate differences.** Incorporate a wide variety of materials, events, and discussions to promote understanding and respect for differences. Recognizing and valuing a variety of cultures, backgrounds, abilities, and perspectives helps all students feel valued and acknowledged, while fostering an environment where everyone's unique qualities are appreciated.
- **Adapt instruction and interventions.** Customize teaching strategies and support to accommodate diverse learning and emotional needs, while still maintaining high learning expectations and experiences for all students. This ensures that every child has access to quality education and promotes success for each student. By tailoring instruction such as offering visual aids, hands-on activities, flexible pacing, or additional emotional support, teachers can better meet individual needs while helping all students achieve their full potential.
- **Train staff on awareness of differences.** Ongoing professional development should include training in anti-bias education, cultural awareness, and protocols to support any students facing harassment, discrimination, or exclusion.
- **Engage families from a variety of backgrounds.** Create relationships and partnerships with families by respecting and acknowledging their values, languages, and cultures. Inclusive family engagement builds trust, strengthens communication, and ensures that all families

feel welcome and involved in their communities, in and out of school.

9.6 LONG-TERM STRATEGIES: CHECK-INS, CULTURE BUILDING, AND ONGOING LEARNING

To create lasting change, schools must commit to consistent practices that support emotional growth, reinforce positive behaviors, and adapt to evolving student needs. The following long-term strategies are recommended to sustain a healthy, inclusive environment over time.

- **Schedule regular emotional check-ins.** Using tools like surveys (for students as well as parents), daily emotional scales, or one-on-one conversations helps assess students' emotional health and identify concerns early. These check-ins create a safe space for students to express feelings, or parents to express concerns, and allow educators to respond with timely support.
- **Celebrate progress.** Acknowledging and celebrating individual achievements and school-wide milestones reinforces positive behavior and builds a sense of pride and belonging. Regular recognition of growth inspires, motivates, and strengthens positive culture.
- **Model empathy and respect.** Adults set the tone. Demonstrating compassion, patience, and respectful communication teaches students how to treat others and upholds community standards. Consistent modeling builds trust, reinforces standards of behavior, and helps create emotionally safe environments.

- **Provide ongoing SEL and mental health education.** Integrating Social- Emotional Learning into lessons and daily routines helps students build self-awareness, empathy, respect, and coping skills. Making SEL a consistent part of the curriculum normalizes emotional development and encourages lifelong well-being.
- **Review and revise policies as needed.** Continuously assessing the effectiveness of anti-bullying policies and updating them to reflect current best practices and recommendations ensures that the most effective protocols remain in place. It also demonstrates the school's commitment to continuous improvement, accountability, and responsiveness to the evolving needs of students and families.

The journey to prevent bullying goes far beyond immediate intervention—it requires ongoing attention to the emotional, psychological, and social well-being of every child.

By addressing mental health, supporting both the bullied and the bully, and embracing inclusive practices, we create a positive culture and lasting change in school, at home, and in the community.

When schools and families commit to working together, building resilience, nurturing empathy, and sustaining long-term support, they help children not only to heal, but to develop the strength and confidence to thrive and stop the bullying cycle.

CHAPTER 10
FINAL THOUGHTS
A UNITED PATH FORWARD TO BREAK THE CYCLE OF BULLYING

Bullying has touched every community, every school, and far too many families in one way or another. It can leave lasting emotional wounds for everyone in the bullying cycle: the bullied, the bully, and even the by-standers. Yet with education, awareness, empathy, and consistent collective action, bullying can be prevented, the cycle of bullying can be broken, and its impact can be greatly reduced.

This guide was created to equip parents, educators, and other influential adults with knowledge, tools, and proven strategies to help foster safe, inclusive, and supportive environments where all children can feel accepted and valued. It draws on a comprehensive body of research and best practices compiled from leading experts, evidence-based programs, and respected organizations from around the globe, in the fields of education, psychology, and bullying prevention.

We began by clarifying what bullying is—addressing common misconceptions and recognizing the many forms it can take, from physical and verbal aggression to subtle social exclusion and cyberbullying. Understanding the dynamics among the bullied, the bully, and the bystander is key to identifying root causes and interrupting harmful cycles.

Equally important is the role of adults. Children watch how we interact, how we respond to conflict, and how we treat others. Whether we are parents, teachers, or community members, our words, actions, and attitudes model the values we instill. The home environment, school culture, and broader community must work together to demonstrate respect, inclusion, and accountability.

Confidence development emerged as a key tool in bully prevention. By helping children build assertiveness, strong communication skills, and a positive internal dialogue, we empower them to stand up for themselves and others. At the same time, fostering empathy and emotional resilience supports children in navigating challenges and building meaningful relationships.

Throughout this guide, we've provided practical strategies for prevention, intervention, and support. From responding effectively when bullying occurs, to setting up safe classroom and home environments, documenting incidents, and using peer-based programs, every action plays a part in shifting the culture.

Real-life case studies emphasized what is possible when families, schools, and communities take a proactive stance. Whether through effective cyberbullying responses, school-wide initiatives, or mental health support, success is within reach when we work together.

We also examined how strong, clearly defined school policies, restorative practices, and collaborative partnerships create a consistent and compassionate approach to bullying prevention. Engaging parents, teachers, students, and community leaders fosters unity and shared responsibility.

In today's digital world, online safety is a growing concern. Teaching responsible digital citizenship at home and at school, setting boundaries, monitoring behavior, and maintaining open conversations help children navigate the internet with confidence and safety.

Finally, long-term change requires a focus on mental health, inclusivity, and sustained support. Recognizing emotional distress, offering counseling when needed, celebrating diversity, and maintaining an ongoing commitment to social-emotional learning are all essential components of a supportive environment at school and at home.

TOGETHER, WE CAN CREATE CHANGE

Bullying prevention and breaking the bullying cycle is not about one single program or policy—it's about collective, consistent, caring relationships and a commitment to protecting the well-being of every child.

As parents, educators, and caring adults, we hold the power to influence hearts, shift behaviors, and build safer spaces. When we work together with intention, compassion, empathy, and shared values, we create schools, homes, and communities where children are not just protected, but empowered to grow safely into confident, kind, and resilient individuals.

Let this guide be a catalyst...an inspiration for reflection, action, and hope. Let's all work together and do our part to create positive change for our children and generations to come. Every child deserves to feel safe. Every voice deserves to be heard...And every act of kindness and compassion can be a turning point for good.

KEEPING THE MOVEMENT ALIVE

Now that you have information, strategies, and tools to understand bullying, build confidence, and take action, it's your turn to help others by sharing your thoughts!

By leaving your honest comments about this book, you will help parents, teachers, students, and others—just like you—find the guidance they may be searching for.

Your words could inspire someone to:

- *take the first step in protecting their child,*
- *create a safer and more positive classroom environment,*
- *or give a student the courage to speak up or stand up for themselves.*

Together, let's raise awareness, break the bully cycle, and create safer, kinder communities for every child.

We are deeply grateful for your support in keeping this mission alive!

WE WANT TO HEAR FROM YOU!

IF YOU ENJOYED THIS BOOK, PLEASE
LEAVE A REVIEW TO HELP OTHERS

https://www.amazon.com/review/review-your-purchases/?asin=
1962863077

Master Method Academy Books

Empowering children, families, and communities through leadership, mindset, and personal growth.

Our publications and programs are designed to inspire transformation from the inside out. Whether you're seeking tools to overcome adversity, unlock your potential, or guide others with purpose, these books offer powerful, practical guidance for every step of your journey.

The Mindset Guide for Winners -
5 Steps to Become a Champion in Your Life

If you want to change your life but don't know how, learn the secrets of Grandmaster Marco Sies' proven 5-Step Master Method system to achieve happiness and success.

ORDER NOW:

This life-changing guide teaches you how to:

✔ Create a bullet proof plan to achieve any goal
✔ Build unshakable and enduring confidence
✔ Create success habits for life
✔ Stay focused, committed and consistent
✔ Condition and strengthen your mind to overcome challenges

⭐⭐⭐⭐⭐ *"A powerful and inspiring book that offers a step-by-step approach to achieving success and abundance in all areas of life."*

"Right from the beginning, this book draws you in and shows you a real life example of how anyone can achieve what they want in life."

Pensamiento Positivo para la Superación Personal - Sabiduría Eterna para el Éxito Moderno

Si quieres cambiar tu vida pero no sabes cómo, aprende los secretos del probado sistema del Método Maestro de 5 Pasos del Gran Maestro Marco Sies para alcanzar la felicidad y el éxito.

ORDENAR AHORA:

Esta guía transformadora te enseña a:

✔ Crea un plan a prueba de balas para lograr cualquier objetivo
✔ Desarrolla una confianza inquebrantable y duradera
✔ Crea hábitos de éxito para toda la vida
✔ Mantente enfocado, comprometido y constante
✔ Acondiciona y fortalece tu mente para superar los desafíos

"¡Me encanta este libro! Me ayudó a superarme en el ámbito personal y laboral."

"¡Me sentí identificado con este libro por el sacrificio y la lucha! ¡Me sentí inspirado en seguir cumpliendo mi sueño, gracias por tus grandes palabras!"

REFERENCES

GOVERNMENT & PUBLIC HEALTH RESOURCES

Centers for Disease Control and Prevention (CDC). (2021). *Preventing Bullying*. https://www.cdc.gov/youth-violence/about/about-bullying.html

U.S. Department of Education. (2019). *Best Practices for Preventing and Addressing Bullying*. https://www.ed.gov

StopBullying.gov. (n.d.). *Respond to Bullying; Prevention Strategies; What You Can Do*. U.S. Department of Health and Human Services. https://www.stopbullying.gov

National Association of School Psychologists (NASP). (2013). *Bullying Prevention and Intervention: Information for Educators*. https://www.nasponline.org

SchoolSafety.gov. (2023). *Bullying Prevention Strategies and Resources for K-12*. https://www.schoolsafety.gov

American Academy of Pediatrics. (n.d.). *Mental Health Screening Tools*. https://www.aap.org

EDUCATIONAL & ADVOCACY ORGANIZATIONS

CASEL (Collaborative for Academic, Social, and Emotional Learning). (2020). *SEL and Bullying Prevention*. https://casel.org

International Institute for Restorative Practices (IIRP). (n.d.). *Restorative Practices Implementation Guide*. https://www.iirp.edu

Common Sense Media. (n.d.). *Digital Safety Guides for Parents and Educators*. https://www.commonsensemedia.org

GLSEN. (2019). *Developing LGBTQ-Inclusive Classroom Curriculum Resource*. https://www.glsen.org

Harvard Graduate School of Education. (n.d.). *How to Build Empathy and Strengthen Your School Community*. https://mcc.gse.harvard.edu

ACADEMIC & RESEARCH-BASED SOURCES

Olweus, D. (1993). *Bullying at School: What We Know and What We Can Do*. Blackwell Publishing.

Dweck, C. S. (2006). *Mindset: The New Psychology of Success*. Random House.

Bandura, A. (1977). *Social Learning Theory*. Prentice Hall.

Holt, M. K., Finkelhor, D., & Kaufman Kantor, G. (2007). *Hidden Forms of Victimization in Elementary Students Involved in Bullying*. School Psychology Review, 36(3), 345–360.

Rigby, K. (2008). *Children and Bullying: How Parents and Educators Can Reduce Bullying at School*. Blackwell Publishing.

Smetana, J. G., & Villalobos, M. (2009). *Social Cognition and Aggression in Adolescence*. In *Bullying, Rejection, and Peer Victimization*, Springer.

Hinduja, S., & Patchin, J. W. (2015). *Bullying Beyond the Schoolyard: Preventing and Responding to Cyberbullying*. Sage Publications.

The University of Chicago Press. (2017). *The Effectiveness of Policy Interventions for School Bullying*. https://www.journals.uchicago.edu

ONLINE TOOLS, CASE STUDIES & PRACTICE-BASED RESOURCES

Cyberbullying Research Center. (n.d.). *Cyberbullying Statistics and Prevention Tips*. https://cyberbullying.org

KidsHealth.org. (n.d.). *Online Safety for Parents*. https://kidshealth.org

GoodTherapy. (n.d.). *Support and Therapy for Bullying*. https://www.goodtherapy.org

Nemours KidsHealth. (n.d.). *Parent–Teacher Conferences: Tips for Teachers*. https://kidshealth.org

American Psychological Association (APA). (n.d.). *Bullying and School Climate*. https://www.apa.org/topics/bullying

American Psychological Association (APA). (2017). *Bullying: What we know based on 40 years of research*. https://www.apa.org/news/press/releases/stress/2017/bullying-report

Mental Health Center Kids. (n.d.). *Empathy Activities for Children*. https://mentalhealthcenterkids.com

PositivePsychology.com. (n.d.). *Self-Esteem Tools for Children*. https://positivepsychology.com

Tom's Guide. (2024). *Best Parental Control Apps*. https://www.tomsguide.com

Kaiser Permanente Thriving Schools. (n.d.). *RISE: Resilience in School Environments*. https://thrivingschools.kaiserpermanente.org

American University School of Education. (n.d.). *Parent–Teacher Communication Strategies*. https://soeonline.american.edu

Core.ac.uk. (n.d.). *Social Learning Theory: Bullying in Schools*. https://core.ac.uk

ERIC. (n.d.). *Bullying Prevention and the Parent Involvement Model*. https://files.eric.ed.gov

"Anti Bullying Quotes for Kids and Students." n.d. White Tiger Karate. Accessed September 1, 2025. https://whitetigerkarate.net/blog/121226/Anti-Bullying-Quotes-for-Kids-and-Students

SUPPORT DIRECTORY

HOTLINES, ADVOCACY GROUPS, AND MENTAL HEALTH RESOURCES

HOTLINES & CRISIS SUPPORT

- **National Bullying Prevention Center - PACER**
  - www.pacer.org/bullying
  - Parent-led support line and resources for children with and without disabilities.
- **988 Suicide & Crisis Lifeline**
  - Call or Text: **988**
  - 988lifeline.org
  - Free, 24/7 confidential support for people in distress, prevention, and crisis resources.
- **Crisis Text Line**
  - Text **HOME** to **741741**
  - www.crisistextline.org
  - Text-based support from trained crisis counselors.

- **SAMHSA's National Helpline**
  - Call: **1-800-662**-HELP (**4357**)
  - www.samhsa.gov
  - Free, confidential support for mental health or substance use issues.
- **The Trevor Project**
  - Call: **1-866-488-7386** | Text: **START** to **678678**
  - www.thetrevorproject.org
  - Crisis support and suicide prevention for LGBTQ+ youth.

MENTAL HEALTH RESOURCES FOR STUDENTS & PARENTS

- **StopBullying.gov**
  - www.stopbullying.gov
  - Government resource with prevention tips, reporting tools, and intervention guidance.
- **Mental Health America (MHA)**
  - www.mhanational.org
  - Free screenings, youth-focused mental health tools, and support.
- **American Academy of Pediatrics (AAP) – Mental Health Minute**
  - www.aap.org
  - Brief videos and tools for pediatric mental health, including bullying and anxiety.
- **Child Mind Institute**
  - www.childmind.org
  - Research-based advice and tools for anxiety, ADHD, bullying, and school-related mental health.

- **KidsHealth by Nemours – For Parents & Kids**
  - www.kidshealth.org
  - Articles and videos on bullying, emotions, digital safety, and school issues.

SUPPORT & RESOURCES FOR TEACHERS AND SCHOOLS

- **International Bullying Prevention Association (IBPA)**
  - www.ibpaworld.org
  - Tools, trainings, and conferences for educators and youth professionals.
- **National PTA – Bullying Resources**
  - www.pta.org/home/programs/connect-for-respect
  - Guides for family-school partnerships to create respectful school climates.
- **Teaching Tolerance (Learning for Justice)**
  - www.learningforjustice.org
  - Anti-bias and anti-bullying lesson plans and professional development.
- **CASEL (Collaborative for Academic, Social, and Emotional Learning)**
  - www.casel.org
  - Leading resource on integrating SEL into schools to reduce bullying and improve mental health.
- **National Association of School Psychologists (NASP)**
  - www.nasponline.org
  - Guidelines on bullying prevention, trauma support, and behavior management.

- **Common Sense Education**
  - www.commonsense.org/education
  - Digital citizenship and cyberbullying curriculum, reviews of apps and parental tools.

www.ingramcontent.com/pod-product-compliance
Lightning Source LLC
Chambersburg PA
CBHW061753120626
46550CB00005B/1977